CHRONICLES OF CANADA

Edited by George M. Wrong and H. H. Langton

In thirty-two volumes

19

PATHFINDERS OF THE GREAT PLAINS

BY LAWRENCE J. BURPEE

Part VI

Pioneers of the North and West

THE BROTHERS LA VÉRENDRYE IN SIGHT OF THE ROCKY MOUNTAINS

JANUARY 1, 1743

From a colour drawing by C. W. Jefferys

PATHFINDERS OF THE GREAT PLAINS

A Chronicle of La Vérendrye and his Sons

BY

LAWRENCE J. BURPEE

EX UNO DISCE OMNES

TORONTO
GLASGOW, BROOK & COMPANY
1915

CONTENTS

ILLUSTRATIONS

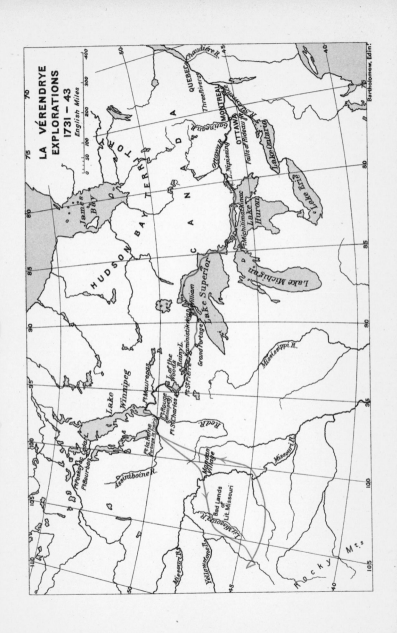

LA VÉRENDRYE
EXPLORATIONS
1731 – 43

English Miles

Bartholomew, Edin.

CHAPTER I

EARLY SERVICE

CANADA has had many brave sons, but none braver than Pierre Gaultier de La Vérendrye, who gave all that he had, including his life, for the glory and welfare of his country. La Vérendrye was born in the quaint little town of Three Rivers, on the St Lawrence, on November 17, 1685. His father was governor of the district of which Three Rivers was the capital; his mother was a daughter of Pierre Boucher, a former governor of the same district. In those days, when Canada was still a French colony, both Three Rivers and Montreal had their own governors, while the whole colony was under the authority of the governor-general, who lived at Quebec.

At that time Three Rivers was a more important place than it is to-day. Next to Quebec and Montreal, it was the largest town in Canada. If we could see it as it was in the days of La Vérendrye, we should find it very different from the towns we know. It was surrounded by a palisade fifteen to eighteen feet high and protected with cannon. The town had always a garrison of regular soldiers, and this garrison was supported in times of necessity by every man and boy in Three Rivers. Those who lived in the neighbourhood were also liable to be called upon for the service of defence. In earlier days, when the dreaded Iroquois might at any moment swoop down upon the little settlement, every man kept his gun within reach, and every man knew how to use it. When the alarm was given, men, women, and children swarmed into Three Rivers, and the town became a secure fortress; for the Indians, ready enough to ambush small parties of white men in the forest or in the fields, rarely dared to attack fortified towns.

In this little walled town Pierre Gaultier de La Vérendrye was born, and spent his boyhood. He was one of ten children, so that he must have had no lack of companions. We have no exact description of the home of the governor of Three Rivers, but it was probably much like that of other seigneurs or landed gentry of New France—a low, rambling, wooden building, with walls solid enough to resist a siege, perhaps a wing or two, many gables, and a lofty roof. It would be flanked, too, with many outhouses. It stood outside the palisades. It must not be supposed, however, that the governor of Three Rivers and his family lived in luxury. People then were obliged to live more simply than they live to-day. The governor had a salary of twelve hundred francs a year, or about two hundred and forty dollars. At that time, it is true, food and clothing were cheaper than they are now, so that this sum would buy a great deal more than it would at the present time; and the governor had other slight resources, for he was able to add to his official income the profits of a small farm and of a trading post on the St Maurice river. Still, it was a small income on which to support a family of ten lusty children, and at the same time keep up the dignity of the position as governor of an important town. Pierre, therefore, like most of the other boys of New France, had to shift for himself at an age when the boys of to-day are still at school.

In those days there was practically only one career for a gentleman's son—that of a soldier. Accordingly we find Pierre entering the army as a cadet at the age of twelve. Nothing is known of his military service up to the year 1704. In that year, however, he took part in an expedition against Deerfield, on the north-western frontier of the colony of Massachusetts. The expedition was commanded by a well-known guerilla leader, Hertel de Rouville, and consisted of about fifty Canadians and two hundred Abnakis and Caughnawagas. These adventurers and redskins were accustomed to all kinds of hardship. In the depth of winter they set out from Montreal to make a journey of nearly three hundred miles. They travelled on snow-shoes through the forest, carrying supplies and provisions on their backs. At the end of a long day's tramp, some comparatively sheltered spot would be found for the camp; the snow would be cleared away with their snow-shoes, and a big camp-fire built in the midst of the clearing. Round this the weary men, white and red, would gather to eat their simple meal and smoke a pipe; then each man would wrap himself in his cloak or blanket and fall asleep, with his feet towards the fire. From time to time some one, warned by the increasing cold, would spring up to throw on the fire another log or two. With the first appearance of dawn, the party would be once more astir; a hasty breakfast would be swallowed, and they would be off again on their long tramp to the south.

So day after day they journeyed until at last, just when they had come to the very end of their provisions, they arrived within sight of the doomed little English frontier village of Deerfield. In the dead of the night Rouville called a halt in a pine forest two miles from the village, and made preparations to surprise the inhabitants. The people of Deerfield were wholly unconscious of the danger from the approach of the French raiders. Although the place had a rude garrison this force was ineffective, since it had little or no discipline. On this particular night even the sentries seem to have found their patrol duty within the palisades of the village so uncomfortable, in the bitter night air, that they had betaken themselves to bed.

Parkman has described the next step :

Rouville and his men, savage with hunger, lay shivering under the pines till about two hours before dawn ; then, leaving their packs and their snow-shoes behind, they moved cautiously towards their prey. There was a crust on the snow strong enough to bear their weight, though not to prevent a rustling noise, as it crunched under the weight of so many men. It is said that from time to time Rouville commanded a halt, in order that the sentinels, if such there were, might mistake the distant sound for rising and falling gusts of wind. In any case, no alarm was given till they had mounted the palisade and dropped silently into the unconscious village. Then with one accord they screeched the war-whoop, and assailed the doors of the houses with axes and hatchets.

The surprised villagers, awakened out of their sleep to find a howling force of French and Indians in their midst, hastily barricaded their doors, and fought desperately with any weapons they could snatch up. In some cases the defenders succeeded in keeping the enemy at bay; but others were not so successful. The French and the Indians hacked openings in the doors and the windows of some of the houses, and through these shot down the inmates. Finally, when day broke, the French had gained possession of most of the village. Then they collected their prisoners and drove them out to their camp in the forest. A few burned houses, a score or so of dead bodies, not only of men but of helpless women and children, and a crowd of shivering prisoners, some of whom were butchered by the way, were the evidences of this inglorious victory.

From the plunder of the houses the victors obtained some provisions which helped to feed their party on the long homeward journey. Before noon of the following day they had started northward again, driving their captives before them through the deep snow. The midwinter tramp through the wilderness proved extremely trying to both the French and their prisoners, but particularly to the prisoners, among whom were many women and children. Many of them were unaccustomed to snowshoes. Yet now they had to make long forced marches in this way over the deep snow. Food, too, was scarce. Some of the prisoners died of starvation; others of exhaustion. Finally the remnant reached the French settlements on the St Lawrence, where they were kindly treated by the inhabitants. Some were afterwards exchanged for French captives in New England, but many never again saw their former homes.

The year after his return from the expedition to Deerfield, Pierre de La Vérendrye took part in another raid against the English settlements. On this occasion, however, the attack was not upon a New England village, but against the town of St John's, in Newfoundland. The expedition was commanded

by an officer named Subercase, who afterwards
became governor of Acadia. St John's was
defended by two forts, with small English
garrisons. The French, who had about four
hundred and fifty soldiers, found themselves
unable to capture the forts. They therefore
abandoned the attack on St John's and returned to the French settlement of Placentia,
burning, as they went, a number of English
fishing villages along the shore.

This kind of warfare could not bring much
honour to a young soldier, and it was probably
joyful news to Pierre to learn that he had been
appointed an ensign in the Bretagne regiment
of the Grenadiers serving in Flanders. He
sailed from Canada in 1707, and for three
years fought with his regiment in what was
known as the War of the Spanish Succession,
in which the English armies were commanded
by the famous Duke of Marlborough. Finally,
at the terrible battle of Malplaquet, in which
thousands of both English and French were
killed, Pierre so distinguished himself that he
won the rank of lieutenant. He received no
less than nine wounds, and was left for dead
upon the field. Fortunately he managed to
escape, to render to his country in the years
to come much greater service.

Finding that there was little hope of further promotion in the French army, since he had no influence in high quarters, Pierre returned to Canada in 1711. After several years in the colonial forces, he abandoned the army, and engaged in the fur trade. As a boy at Three Rivers, he had enjoyed many chances of meeting the fur-traders who came down to the little town on the St Lawrence with their packs of valuable peltry, and had shown an especial and fascinated interest in their stories of the boundless country that lay north and west of the string of settlements on the St Lawrence. This country was so vast in extent that even the most remote tribes yet visited by the white traders could state nothing definite as to its outer boundaries, though, in answer to the eager questions of the white men, they invented many untrue tales about it.

The fur-traders themselves were divided into two classes. The more staid and respectable class built trading forts in the interior on the borders of territories occupied by the Indians. Here they kept a supply of the things required by the natives : guns, powder and balls, tobacco, blankets, bright-coloured cotton, axes and small tools, flints and steels, vermilion for war-paint, and beads of every colour and de-

scription.   The Indians brought their furs into
the forts and bartered them for the goods
that they needed.   Sometimes, with no sense
of real values, they traded beaver skins and
other pelts of high worth for a piece of gaudy
cotton, a little vermilion, or a handful of
beads.   The white men, of course, brought
things which rapidly became indispensable to
the Indians, whose native bows and arrows
and hatchets of stone seemed almost useless
compared with the muskets and the steel
axes brought from Europe.   To acquire these
things became vital to the Indians, and the
traders who now supplied them acquired each
year thousands of beautiful furs.   These were
tied up securely into packs and carried in
canoes down to Montreal or Three Rivers,
where they were bought by the great merchants
and sent by ship to France.   The furs that
had been bought from the Indian for a mere
trifle fetched hundreds of francs when they
finally reached Paris.

The second class of traders, known as
coureurs de bois, or wood-runners, were very
different from the first.   Speaking generally,
they were young men, sometimes of good
family, who found life in the older towns and
settlements prosaic and uninteresting, and when

they went to the interior did not care to be
tied down to the humdrum existence of the
trading forts.   Instead of requiring the Indians
to bring their furs down to some fort, these
enterprising rovers of the forest went into the
Indian country. Sometimes they took light
trading goods with them to barter with the
redskins for furs, but oftener they themselves
hunted and trapped the beaver, the otter, and
the fox. The coureurs de bois were generally
men of reckless courage, ready to face danger
and hardship. From long living among the
savages they themselves became in time half
savage. Some of them took Indian wives and
were adopted into the tribes.

When one of these wood-runners had obtained a quantity of furs, he made them up
into packs, loaded them carefully in his canoe,
and set out for the distant settlements, Montreal,
Three Rivers, or Quebec. He knew the wild
northern streams as well as any Indian ; he
could run his canoe safely down a rapid where
an inch one way or the other would dash it
against the rocks ; and he could paddle all day
with only an occasional stop for a meal or a
smoke. When he came to an impassable rapid
or waterfall, he beached his canoe and carried
everything—canoe, packs, gun, and provisions

—overland to the navigable water ahead. At night he pulled his canoe ashore, built a camp-fire, and cooked over the flames a partridge, a wild duck, or a venison steak. If he had not been fortunate enough to meet with such game, he made a simple meal of pemmican—dried venison mixed with fat—a supply of which he always carried in a bag in case of need. Then he smoked his pipe, rolled himself in his blanket, placed his gun within reach, and slept soundly until the sun awakened him on the following morning. When he reached the far-off towns on the St Lawrence, he traded part of his furs for any goods which he needed, and was only too likely to get rid of the rest in dissipation. As soon as his money was spent, he would turn his back on civilization and live once more the wild life of the Indian country.

From such men as these, who were con-stantly to be seen in the little town of Three Rivers, Pierre de La Vérendrye heard many stories of the wonderful country that lay far towards the setting sun. They told him of mighty rivers and great lakes. Some of these they had seen; others they had heard of from the Indians. Always the young man heard rumours of a great *Mer de l'Ouest*, or Western

Sea, which French explorers had been seeking ardently ever since the days of Jacques Cartier and Samuel Champlain. In the earlier days, when the French first came to Canada, this Western Sea was supposed to be somewhere above Montreal. Probably the Indians who first spoke of it to Jacques Cartier meant nothing more than Lake Ontario. Then, in the days of Champlain, the sea was sought farther westward. Champlain heard rumours of a great water beyond the Ottawa river. He paddled up the Ottawa, reached Lake Nipissing, and, descending what is now known as French River, found the immense body of water of which the Indians had told him. He had discovered Lake Huron, but this, again, was not the Western Sea. Other explorers, following in his footsteps, discovered Lake Michigan and Lake Superior; but still neither of these was the Western Sea. So, in La Vérendrye's day, men were dreaming of a Western Sea somewhere beyond Lake Superior. How far was it westward of Lake Superior? Who could tell? The Indians were always ready with a plausible tale, and many believed that the Western Sea would still be found at no great distance beyond the uppermost of the Great Lakes.

La Vérendrye was a young man of ambition
and imagination. The spirit of adventure
called him to a great exploit in discovery, as
it had called earlier explorers French in blood—
Jacques Cartier and Champlain and Radisson,
Nicolet and Etienne Brulé, Marquette and La
Salle. They one and all had sought diligently
for the Western Sea; they had made many
notable discoveries, but in this one thing they
all had failed. La Vérendrye determined to
strive even more earnestly than any of his great
predecessors to discover a way to the Western
Sea, not so much for his own advantage as
for the honour and glory of his native country.
This great idea had been taking form in his
mind from the days of his early boyhood,
when, seated before the great log fire in his
father's home in Three Rivers, he had first
listened to the stirring tales of the wood-
runners.

Years went by, however, before any means
appeared whereby his ambition might be
realized. In 1712, after his return from
France, he had married the daughter of a
Canadian named Dandonneau and had made
his home on the island of Dupas in the
St Lawrence, near Three Rivers. Here four
sons were born to him, all of whom were

later to accompany their father on his
western explorations. His principal occupa-
tion at this time was to look after the trading-
post of La Gabelle on the St Maurice river,
not far from the point where it discharges its
waters into the St Lawrence.

La Vérendrye's experience and capacity as
a fur-trader, gained at this post of La Gabelle,
led the governor of the colony to offer him,
in the year 1726, the command of an important
trading fort on Lake Nipigon, north of Lake
Superior. With his great project of western
exploration always in mind, he eagerly accepted
the offer. For three or four years he remained
in command of the Nipigon post, faithfully
discharging his duties as a fur-trader, but
with his mind always alert for any information that might help him later to discover a
way to the Western Sea.

One day there came to him from the
Kaministikwia river — on which the city of
Fort William now stands—an Indian named
Ochagach. According to his own story,
Ochagach had travelled far towards the setting
sun, until he came to a great lake, out of which
a river flowed westward. He said that he
had paddled down this river until he reached
a point where the water ebbed and flowed.

Through fear of the savage tribes that inhabited the shores of the river, he had not gone to its mouth, but he had been told that the river emptied into a great salt lake or sea, upon the coasts of which dwelt men of terrifying mien, who lived in fortified towns ; he had been told that these men wore armour and rode on horseback, and that great ships visited the towns which they had built on the coasts.

Ochagach's story made a deep impression on La Vérendrye. Not that he accepted the whole account as true. He knew too well the wild imagination of the Indian, and his delight in telling marvellous tales to the white men. But the river that flowed westward and fell into a great sea answered so closely to his own dream, and seemed on the whole so probable, that he was persuaded of the truth of the story. He determined, therefore, to surrender his command of the Nipigon post and to equip an expedition for the discovery of the Western Sea, which now seemed to be within comparatively easy reach. To do this, he must obtain the permission and support of the governor-general of Canada, the Marquis de Beauharnois. He therefore set out for Quebec, taking with him a rough map which Ochagach had drawn for him. This map professed to make clear the position of the countries which Ochagach declared that he had visited.

The governor at Quebec was keenly interested in these plans for western discovery, and wrote immediately to the French king, urging that La Vérendrye should be provided with one hundred men and the necessary supplies and equipment. But King Louis at this time was deeply engaged in European wars and intrigues and could not spare any money for the work of exploration. All that he would grant was a monopoly of the western fur trade. That is to say, La Vérendrye was to be allowed to build trading forts in the country which he was about to explore, and, out of the profits of his traffic with the Indians, he might pay the cost of his expedition to the Western Sea. No other French traders would be permitted to trade in this part of the country.

This was sorry encouragement to a man whose only desire was to bring glory and honour to his native country ; but it was all that could be hoped for from the government or the king. La Vérendrye was too true a leader to abandon plans merely because the road was not made easy for him. As the king would not pay the cost of his expedition, he

made up his mind to find help from some other
source. He must have men; he must have
canoes, provisions, and goods to trade with the
natives. All this demanded a great deal of
money. He devoted at once to the cause his
own little fortune, but this was far from
sufficient. Off he went to Montreal, to plead
with its merchants to help him. The
merchants, however, were not much interested
in his plans for western discovery. They were
business men without patriotism; they looked
for something that would bring profit, not
for what might advance the interests of their
country.

It thus happened that if La Vérendrye had
had nothing to offer them but the opportunity
of sharing in the distinction of his great discovery, they would have turned deaf ears to
his appeal, no matter how eloquent he might
have been. But he was too shrewd a man to
urge plans to which he knew the merchants
would not listen. He could turn the king's
monopoly to good account. 'Give me money
to pay my men,' he said, 'and goods to trade
with the western tribes, and I will bring you
rich returns in beaver skins. No other traders
are permitted to go into the country west of
Lake Superior. I will build trading forts

there.   From these as a base I will continue
my search for the Western Sea.   All the profits
of the enterprise, the rich furs that are
brought into my posts, shall be yours.'   Here
was something that the self-seeking merchants
could understand.   They saw in the fur-
trading monopoly a chance of a golden harvest,
a return of hundreds for every franc that they
advanced towards the expenses of the under-
taking.   With cheerful haste, therefore, they
agreed to pay the cost of the expedition.   La
Vérendrye was delighted and lost no time in
employing such persons as he needed—soldiers,
canoe-men, and hunters.   Birch-bark canoes
were procured and laden with provisions,
equipment, and packages of goods to trade
with the Indians ; and in the early summer of
1731 all was ready for the great western
journey.   With La Vérendrye were to go three
of his sons, Jean-Baptiste, Pierre, and François,
and his nephew La Jemeraye.   A Jesuit
missionary, Father Messager, would join the
party at Fort Michilimackinac, and the Indian
Ochagach was to act as guide.

CHAPTER II

As La Vérendrye led his men from the gates of
Montreal to the river where waited his little
fleet of birch-bark canoes, his departure was
watched with varied and conflicting emotions.
In the crowd that surrounded him were friends
and enemies ; some who openly applauded
his design, others who less openly scoffed at
it ; priests exhorting him to devote all his
energies to furthering the missionary aims of
their Church among the wild tribes of the West ;
jealous traders commenting among themselves
upon the injustice involved in granting a
monopoly of the western fur trade to this
scheming adventurer ; partners in the enterprise anxiously watching the loading of the
precious merchandise they had advanced to
him, and wondering whether their cast of the
dice would bring fortune or failure ; busy-
bodies bombarding him with advice ; and a
crowd of idle onlookers, divided in their minds

as to whether La Vérendrye would return triumphantly from the Western Sea laden with the spoils of Cathay and Cipango, or would fall a victim to the half-human monsters that were reputed to inhabit the wilderness of the West.

But now everything was ready. La Vérendrye gave the word of command, and the canoes leaped forward on their long voyage. A new search for the Western Sea had begun. No man knew how it would end. The perils and hardships encountered by the discoverers of America in crossing the Atlantic were much less terrible than those with which La Vérendrye and his men must battle in exploring the boundless plains of the unknown West. The voyage across the sea would occupy but a few weeks; this journey by inland waterways and across the illimitable spaces of the western prairies would take many months and even years. There was a daily menace from savage foes lurking on the path of the adventurers. Hardy and dauntless must they be who should return safely from such a quest. Little those knew who stood enviously watching the departure of the expedition what bitter tribute its leader must pay to the relentless gods of the Great Plains for his hardihood in invading their savage domain.

The way lay up the broad and picturesque Ottawa, rich even then with the romantic history of a century of heroic exploits. This was the great highway between the St Lawrence and the Upper Lakes for explorers, missionaries, war parties, and traders. Up this stream, one hundred and eighteen years before, Champlain had pushed his way, persuaded by the ingenious impostor Nicolas Vignau that here was the direct road to Cathay. At St Anne's the expedition made a brief halt to ask a blessing on the enterprise. Here the men, according to custom, each received a dram of liquor. When they had again taken their places, paddles dipped at the word of command, and, like a covey of birds, the canoes skimmed over the dark waters of the Ottawa, springing under the sinewy strokes of a double row of paddlers against the swift current of the river. Following the shore closely, they made rapid progress up-stream. At noon they landed on a convenient island, where they quickly kindled a fire. A pot of tea was swung above it from a tripod. With jest and story the meal went on, and as soon as it was finished they were again afloat, paddling vigorously and making quick time. Sunset approached— the brief but indescribably beautiful sunset of a Canadian summer. The sun sank behind the maples and cedars, and a riot of colour flooded the western horizon. Rainbow hues swept up half-way to the zenith, waving, mingling, changing from tint to tint, as through the clouds flamed up the last brightness of the sinking sun. A rollicking chorus sank away on the still air, and the men gazed for a moment upon a scene which, however familiar, could never lose its charm. The song of the birds was hushed. All nature seemed to pause. Then as the outermost rim of the sun dropped from sight, and the brilliant colouring of a moment ago toned to rose and saffron, pink and mauve, the world moved on again, but with a seemingly subdued motion. The voyageurs resumed their song, but the gay chorus that had wakened echoes from the overhanging cliffs,

En roulant ma boule,
Rouli, roulant, ma boule roulant,
En roulant ma boule roulant,
En roulant ma boule,

was changed to the pathetic refrain of a song then as now dear to the heart of French Canadians—*A la claire fontaine.*

In the cool twilight the men paddled on, placing mile after mile between them and

Montreal. Presently the river widened into a lakelike expanse. The moon rose and shot its soft gleam across the water. No ripple stirred the smooth surface, save where the paddles dipped and the prow of each canoe cut like a knife through the stream. Belated birds flew overhead, making for home. A stag broke through the bushes on the farther shore, caught sight of the canoes, gazed at them for a moment, and then disappeared. It was growing late when La Vérendrye, from the foremost canoe, gave the word to camp. The canoes turned shoreward, lightly touching the shelving bank, and the men sprang nimbly to the land. Fires were lighted, the tents were pitched, and everything was made snug for the night. The hunters had not been idle during the day, and a dozen brace of birds were soon twirling merrily on the spit, while venison steaks added appetizing odours.

Their hunger satisfied, the men lounged about on the grass, smoking and listening to the yarns of some famous story-teller. He would tell them, perhaps, the pathetic story of Cadieux, who, on this very stream, had held the dreaded Iroquois at bay while his comrades escaped. Cadieux himself escaped the Iroquois, only to fall a victim to the *folie des bois*, or madness of the woods, wandering aimlessly in circles, until, famished and exhausted, he lay down to die. When his comrades returned in search of him, they found beside him a birch bark on which he had written his death chant :

> Thou little rock of the high hill, attend !
> Hither I come this last campaign to end !
> Ye echoes soft, give ear unto my sigh ;
> In languishing I speedily shall die.
>
> Dear little birds, your dulcet harmony
> What time you sing makes this life dear to me.
> Ah ! had I wings that I might fly like you ;
> Ere two days sped I should be happy too.

Then, as the camp-fires sank into heaps of glowing embers, each man would wrap his blanket about him and with kind mother earth for his pillow and only the dome of heaven above him, would sleep as only those may whose resting-place is in the free air of the wilderness.

At sunrise they were once more away, on a long day's paddle up-stream. They passed the Long Sault, where long before the heroic Dollard and his little band of Frenchmen held at bay a large war party of Iroquois—sacrificing their lives to save the little struggling colony at Montreal. Again, their way lay beneath those towering cliffs overlooking the Ottawa, on which now stand the Canadian Houses of

Parliament.   They had just passed the curtain-
like falls of the Rideau on one side, and the
mouth of the turbulent Gatineau on the other,
and before them lay the majestic Chaudière.
Here they disembarked. The voyageurs, following the Indian example, threw a votive offer-
ing of tobacco into the boiling cauldron, for
the benefit of the dreaded Windigo.   Then,
shouldering canoes and cargo, they made their
way along the portage to the upper stream,
and, launching and reloading the canoes, pro-
ceeded on their journey.   So the days passed,
each one carrying them farther from the
settlements and on, ever on, towards the unknown West, and perhaps to the Western Sea.

From the upper waters of the Ottawa they
carried their canoes over into a series of small
lakes and creeks that led to Lake Nipissing, and
thence they ran down the French river to
Lake Huron.   Launching out fearlessly on
this great lake, they paddled swiftly along the
north shore to Fort Michilimackinac, where
they rested for a day or two.   Fort Michilimackinac was on the south side of the strait
which connects Lake Huron and Lake
Michigan, and lay so near the water that the
waves frequently broke against the stockade.
Passing through the gates, above which floated

the fleurs-de-lis of France, they found themselves in an enclosure, some two acres in
extent, containing thirty houses and a small
church. On the bastions stood in a conspicu-
ous position two small brass cannon, captured
from the English at Fort Albany on Hudson
Bay, in 1686, by De Troyes and Iberville.[1]

It was now the end of July, and La Vérendrye had still a long way to go. After a
brief rest, he gathered his party together, em-
barked once more, and steered his way on that
great inland sea, Lake Superior. All that had
gone before was child's play to what must now
be encountered. In contrast to the blue and
placid waters of Lake Huron, the explorers now
found themselves in the midst of a dark and
sombre sea, whose waves, seldom if ever still,
could on occasion rival the Atlantic in their
fierce tumult. Even in this hottest month of the
year the water was icy cold, and the keen wind
that blew across the lake forced those who were
not paddling to put on extra clothing. They
must needs be hardy and experienced voyageurs
who could safely navigate these mad waters in
frail bark canoes. Slowly they made their way
along the north shore, buffeted by storms and in
constant peril of their lives, until at last, on

[1] See The 'Adventurers of England' on Hudson Bay, pages 73-88.

August 26, they reached the Grand Portage, near the mouth of the Pigeon river, or about fifteen leagues south-west of Fort Kaministikwia, where the city of Fort William now stands.

La Vérendrye would have pushed on at once for Lac la Pluie, or Rainy Lake, where he purposed to build the first of his western posts, but when he ordered his men to make the portage there was first deep muttering, and then open mutiny. Two or three of the boatmen, bribed by La Vérendrye's enemies at Montreal, had drawn such terrible pictures of the horrors before them, and had so played upon the fears of their superstitious comrades, that these now refused flatly to follow their leader into the unhallowed and fiend-infested regions which lay beyond. The hardships they had already endured, and the further hardships of the long and difficult series of portages which lay between them and Rainy Lake, also served to dishearten the men. Some of them, however, had been with La Jemeraye at Lake Pepin, on the Mississippi, and were not to be dismayed. These La Vérendrye persuaded to continue the exploration. The others gradually weakened in their opposition, and at last it was agreed that La Jemeraye, with half the men, should go on to Rainy Lake and build a fort there, while La Vérendrye, with the other half, should spend the winter at Kaministikwia, and keep the expedition supplied with provisions.

In this way the winter passed. The leader was, we may be sure, restless at the delay and impatient to advance farther. The spring brought good news. Late in May La Jemeraye returned from Rainy Lake, bringing canoes laden with valuable furs, the result of the winter's traffic. These were immediately sent on to Michilimackinac, for shipment to the partners at Montreal. La Jemeraye reported that he had built a fort at the foot of a series of rapids, where Rainy Lake discharges into the river of the same name. He had built the fort in a meadow, among groves of oak. The lake teemed with fish, and the woods which lined its shores were alive with game, large and small. The picture was one to make La Vérendrye even more eager to advance. On June 8 he set out with his entire party for Fort St Pierre, as the new establishment had been named, to commemorate his own name of Pierre. It took a month to traverse the intricate chain of small lakes and streams, with their many portages, connecting Lake Superior and Rainy Lake.

After a short rest at Fort St Pierre, La Vérendrye pushed on rapidly, escorted in state by fifty canoes of Indians, to the Lake of the Woods. Here he built a second post, Fort St Charles, on a peninsula running out far into the lake on the south-west side—an admirable situation, both for trading purposes and for defence. This fort he describes as consisting of ' an enclosure made with four rows of posts, from twelve to fifteen feet in height, in the form of an oblong square, within which are a few rough cabins constructed of logs and clay, and covered with bark.'

In the spring of 1735 Father Messager returned to Montreal, and with him went La Jemeraye, to report the progress already made. He described to the governor the difficulties they had encountered, and urged that the king should be persuaded to assume the expense of further explorations towards the Western Sea. The governor could, however, do nothing.

Meanwhile Jean, La Vérendrye's eldest son, had advanced still farther and had made his way to Lake Winnipeg. He took with him a handful of toughened veterans, and tramped on snow-shoes through the frozen forest—four hundred and fifty miles in the stern midwinter

of a region bitterly cold. Near the mouth of
the Winnipeg river, where it empties into Lake
Winnipeg, they found an ideal site for the fort
which they intended to build. Immediately
they set to work, felled trees, drove stout stakes
into the frozen ground for a stockade, put up a
rough shelter inside, and had everything ready
for La Vérendrye's arrival in the spring. They
named the post Fort Maurepas, in honour of a
prominent minister of the king in France at
the time.

La Vérendrye had now carried out, and more
than carried out, the agreement made with the
governor Beauharnois. He had established a
chain of posts—strung like beads on a string
—from Lake Superior to Lake Winnipeg, from
the river Kaministikwia to the open prairie.
But the distance he had traversed, the difficulties he had encountered, and, above all,
the expense incurred, had been far in excess
of anything he had anticipated. These were
discouraging experiences. He seemed at last
to have reached the limit of his resources and
endurance. To advance farther with the
slender means now at his command seemed
almost impossible. Should he turn back?
His men were more than willing. Every
step eastward would bring them nearer their

homes, their families, and the pleasures and
dissipations of the Canadian towns on the far-
off St Lawrence. To turn back was the easiest
thing for them. But it was not easy for a
man like La Vérendrye. To return meant
failure ; and for him there was no such thing
as failure while health and strength endured.
At whatever cost, he must push on towards the
Western Sea.

The situation was nevertheless most critical.
His own means had long since been exhausted.
True, he possessed a monopoly of the fur
trade, but what did it profit him ? He had not
touched, and never would be able to touch,
a franc of the proceeds : the shrewd merchants
of Montreal had made sure of this. To La
Vérendrye the monopoly was simply a mill-
stone added to the burdens he was already
forced to bear. It did not increase his resources ; it delayed his great enterprise ; and
it put an effective weapon in the hands of his
enemies. Little cause had he to be grateful
for the royal monopoly. He would have in-
finitely preferred the direct grant of even a score
of capable, well-equipped men. These, main-
tained at the king's expense, he might lead by
the quickest route to the Western Sea.

As it was, the merchants in Montreal refused

to send up further supplies ; his men remained
unpaid ; he even lacked a sufficient supply of
food. There was nothing for it but to turn
back, make the long journey to Montreal and
Quebec, and there do his utmost to arrange
matters. He had already sunk from 40,000
to 50,000 livres in the enterprise. In all
justice, the king should assume the expense of
further explorations in quest of the Great Sea.
The governor, the Marquis de Beauharnois,
shared this view, and had already pressed
the court to grant La Vérendrye the assistance
he so urgently needed. ' The outlay,' he
wrote to the king's minister, Maurepas, ' will
not be great ; the cost of the *engagés* [hired
men] for three years, taking into account
what can be furnished from the king's stores,
would not exceed 30,000 livres at most.' The
king, however, refused to undertake the expense of the expedition. Those who had
assumed the task should, he thought, be in a
position to continue it by means of the profits
derived from their monopoly of the fur trade.
The facts did not justify the royal view of
the matter. La Vérendrye had enjoyed the
monopoly for two or three years—with the
result that he was now very heavily, indeed
alarmingly, in debt.

His was not a nature, however, to be crushed by either indifference or opposition. He had reached the parting of the ways. Nothing was to be hoped for from the court. He must either abandon his enterprise or continue it at his own risk and expense. He went to Montreal and saw his partners. With infinite patience he suffered their unjust reproaches. He was neglecting their interests, they grumbled. The profits were not what they had a right to expect. He thought too much of the Western Sea and not enough of the beavers. He was a dreamer, and they were practical men of business.

What could La Vérendrye say that would have weight with men of this stamp? Should he tell them of the glory that would accrue to his and their country by the discovery of the Western Sea? At this they would only shrug their shoulders. Should he tell them of the unseen forces that drew him to that wonderful land of the West—where the crisp clear air held an intoxicating quality unknown in the East; where the eye roamed on and on over limitless expanses of waving green, till the mind was staggered at the vastness of the prospect; where the very largeness of nature seemed to enter into a man and to crush out things petty and selfish ? In doing this he would be beating the air. They were incapable of understanding him. They would deem him mad.

Crushing down, therefore, both his enthusiasm for the western land and his anger at their dulness, he met the merchants of Montreal on their own commercial level. He told them that the posts he had established were in the very heart of the fur country ; that the Assiniboines and Crees had engaged to bring large quantities of beaver skins to the forts ; that the northern tribes were already turning from the English posts of the Hudson's Bay Company in the Far North to the more accessible posts of the French ; that the richly watered and wooded country between Kaministikwia and Lake Winnipeg abounded in every description of fur-bearing animal ; that over the western prairies roamed the buffalo in vast herds which seemed to blacken the green earth as far as eye could reach. His eloquence over the outlook for trade proved convincing. As he painted the riches of the West in terms that appealed with peculiar force to these traders in furs, their hostility melted away. The prospect of profit at the rate of a hundred per cent once more filled them with enthusiasm. They agreed to equip the expedition anew. It thus happened that when the intrepid explorer again turned his face towards the West, fortune seemed to smile once more. His canoes were loaded with a second equipment for the posts of the Western Sea. Perhaps at that moment it seemed to him hardly to matter that he was in debt deeper than ever.

While in the East completing these arrangements, La Vérendrye took steps to ensure that his youngest son, Louis, now eighteen years of age, should join the other members of the family engaged in the work. The boy was to be taught how to prepare maps and plans, so that, when he came west in the following year, he might be of material assistance to the expedition. The explorer would then have his four sons and his nephew in the enterprise.

The hopeful outlook did not long endure. It was soon clear that La Vérendrye had again to meet trials which should try his mettle still more severely. Shortly after his return to Fort St Charles on the Lake of the Woods, his son Jean arrived from Fort Maurepas, with evil news indeed. La Jemeraye, his nephew and chief lieutenant, whose knowledge of the western tribes was invaluable, whose en-

thusiasm for the great project was only second
to his own, whose patience and resourceful-
ness had helped the expedition out of many
a tight corner—La Jemeraye was dead. He
had remained in harness to the last, and had
laboured day and night, in season and out of
season, pushing explorations in every direction,
meeting and conciliating the Indian tribes,
building up the fur trade at the western posts.
Though sorely needing rest, he had toiled on
uncomplainingly, with no thought that he was
showing heroism, till at last his overtaxed
body collapsed and he died almost on his feet—
the first victim of the search for the Western Sea.

Meanwhile the little garrison at Fort St
Charles was almost at the point of starvation.
La Vérendrye had travelled ahead at such
rapid speed that his supplies were still a long
way in the rear when he reached the fort.
In face of the pressing need, it was decided
to send a party down to meet the boats at
Kaministikwia and to fetch back at once the
supplies which were most urgently required.
Jean, now twenty-three years of age, was
placed in charge of the expedition, and with
him went the Jesuit missionary, Father
Aulneau, on his way down to Fort Michilimackinac. The day for departure was named,

and everything was made ready the night
before so that there might be no delay in starting early in the morning.   The sun had hardly
risen above the horizon and was yet filtering
through the dense foliage of pine and cedar,
when Jean de La Vérendrye and his men em-
barked and pushed off from the shore.   The
paddles dipped almost noiselessly, and the three
light canoes skimmed lightly over the surface
of the Lake of the Woods, followed by shouts
of farewell from the fort.

For a time the party skirted the shore.
Then they struck out boldly across the lake.
The melodies of the forest followed them for
a time, and then died away in the distance.
Nothing was now to be heard but the dip of
paddles and the soft swirl of eddies flying
backward from either side of the canoes.   The
morning sun swept across the lake ; a faint
breeze stirred a ripple on the surface of the
water.   From far away came faintly the laugh
of a solitary loon.   The men paddled strenu-
ously, with minds intent upon nothing more
serious than the halt for breakfast.   The priest
was lost in meditation.   Jean de La Vérendrye
sat in the foremost canoe, with eyes alert,
scanning the horizon as the little flotilla drew
rapidly across the lake.

At the same time, approaching from the opposite direction, was a fleet of canoes manned by a hundred savages, the fierce and implacable Sioux of the prairie. They had reached the Lake of the Woods by way of a stream that bore the significant name *The Road of War*. This was the war-path of the Sioux from their own country, south of what is now the province of Manitoba, to the country of the Chippewas and the Crees farther east. Whenever the Sioux followed this route, they were upon no peaceful errand. As the Sioux entered the lake, a mist was rising slowly from the water ; but before it completely hid their canoes a keen-sighted savage saw the three canoes of the French, who were about to land on the far side of an island out in the lake. Cautiously the Sioux felt their way across to the near side of the island, and landed unperceived. They glided noiselessly through the thick underbrush, and, as they approached the other shore, crept from tree to tree, finally wriggling snake-wise to the very edge of the thicket. Beneath them lay a narrow beach, on which some of the voyageurs had built a fire to prepare the morning meal. Others lay about, smoking and chatting idly. Jean de La Vérendrye sat a little apart, perhaps

recording the scanty particulars of the journey.
The Jesuit priest walked up and down, deep in
his breviary.

The circumstances could hardly have been
more favourable for the sudden attack which
the savages were eager to make. The French
had laid aside their weapons, or had left them
behind in the canoes. They had no reason
to expect an attack. They were at peace with
the western tribes—even with those Ishmaelites
of the prairie, the Sioux. Presently a twig
snapped under the foot of a savage. Young
La Vérendrye turned quickly, caught sight of
a waving plume, and shouted to his men.
Immediately from a hundred fierce throats
the war-whoop rang out. The Sioux leaped
to their feet. Arrows showered down upon
the French. Jean, Father Aulneau, and a
dozen voyageurs fell. The rest snatched up
their guns and fired. Several of the Sioux, who
had incautiously left cover, fell. The odds
were, however, overwhelmingly against the
French. They must fight in the open, while the
Indians remained comparatively secure among
the trees. The French made an attempt to reach
the canoes, but had to abandon it, for the
Sioux now completely commanded the approach and no man could reach the water alive.

The surviving French, now reduced to half a dozen, retreated down the shore. With yells of triumph the Sioux followed, keeping within shelter of the trees. In desperation the voyageurs dropped their guns and took to the water, hoping to be able to swim to a neighbouring island. This was a counsel of despair, for wounded and exhausted as they were, the feat was impossible. When the Sioux rushed down to the shore, they realized the plight of the French, and did not even waste an arrow on them. One by one the swimmers sank beneath the waves. After watching their tragic fate, the savages returned to scalp those who had fallen at the camp. With characteristic ferocity they hacked and mutilated the bodies. Then, gathering up their own dead, they hastily retreated by the way they had come.

For some time it was not known why the Sioux had made an attack, seemingly unprovoked, upon the French. Gradually, however, it leaked out that earlier in the year a party of Sioux on their way to Fort St Charles on a friendly visit had been fired upon by a party of Chippewas. The Sioux had shouted indignantly, 'Who fire on us?' and the Chippewas, in ambush, had yelled back with grim humour, 'The French.' The Sioux retreated, vowing a terrible vengeance against the treacherous white men. Their opportunity came even sooner than they had expected. A trader named Bourassa, who had left Fort St Charles for Michilimackinac shortly before the setting out of Jean de La Vérendrye and his party, had camped for the night on the banks of the Rainy river. The following morning, as he was about to push off from the shore, he was surrounded by thirty canoes manned by a hundred Sioux. They bound him hand and foot, tied him to a stake, and were about to burn him alive when a squaw who was with him sprang forward to defend him. Fortunately for him his companion had been a Sioux maiden; she had been captured by a war party of Monsones some years before and rescued from them by Bourassa. She knew of the projected journey of Jean de La Vérendrye. 'My kinsmen,' she now cried, 'what are you about to do? I owe my life to this Frenchman. He has done nothing but good to me. Why should you destroy him? If you wish to be revenged for the attack made upon you, go forward and you will meet twenty-four Frenchman, with whom is the son of the chief who killed your people.'

Bourassa was too much frightened to oppose

the statement. In his own account of what happened he is, indeed, careful to omit any mention of this particular incident. The Sioux released Bourassa, after taking possession of his arms and supplies. Then they paddled down to the lake, where they were only too successful in finding the French and in making them the victims of the cruel joke of the Chippewas.

This murder of his son was the most bitter blow that had yet fallen upon La Vérendrye. But he betrayed no sign of weakness. Not even the loss of his son was sufficient to turn him back from his search for the Western Sea. ' I have lost,' he writes simply to Maurepas, ' my son, the reverend Father, and my Frenchmen, misfortunes which I shall lament all my life.' Some comfort remained. The great explorer still had three sons, ready and willing like himself to sacrifice their lives for the glory of New France.

CHAPTER III

ACROSS THE PLAINS

FOR several years La Vérendrye had been hearing wonderful accounts of a tribe of Indians in the West who were known as the Mandans. Wherever he went, among the Chippewas, the Crees, or the Assiniboines, some one was sure to speak of the Mandans, and the stories grew more and more marvellous. La Vérendrye knew that Indians were very much inclined to exaggerate. They would never spoil a good story by limiting it to what they knew to be true. They liked a joke as well as other people ; and, when they found that the white men who visited them were eager to know all about the country and the tribes of the far interior, they invented all sorts of impossible stories, in which truth and fiction were so mingled that at length the explorers did not know what to believe.

Much that was told him by the Indians concerning the Mandans La Vérendrye knew

could not possibly be true ; he thought that
some of their stories were probably correct.
The Indians said that the Mandans were
white like himself, that they dressed like Europeans, wore armour, had horses and cattle,
cultivated the ground, and lived in fortified
towns. Their home was described as being
far towards the setting sun, on a great river
that flowed into the ocean. La Vérendrye
knew that the Spaniards had made settlements on the western coast of America, and
he thought that the mysterious strangers
might perhaps be Spaniards. At any rate
they seemed to be white men, and, if the
Indian stories were even partially true, they
would be able to show him that way to
the great water which it was the ambition
of his life to find. His resolve, therefore,
was inevitable. He would visit these white
strangers, whoever they might be ; and he had
great hopes that they would be able to guide
him to the object of his quest.

For some time, however, he was not able to
carry out this intended visit to the Mandans.
The death of his nephew La Jemeraye, followed
soon after by the murder of his son Jean, upset
all his plans for a time. Further, he had great
difficulty in keeping peace among the Indian

tribes.   The Chippewas and the Crees, who had
always been friendly to the French, were in-
dignant at the treacherous massacre of the
white men by the Sioux, and urged La Vérendrye to lead a war party against this enemy.
La Vérendrye not only refused to do this himself, but he told them that they must on no
account go to war with the Sioux.   He warned
them that their Great Father, the king of
France, would be very angry with them if they
disobeyed his commands.   Had they not known
him so well, the Indians would have despised
La Vérendrye as a coward for refusing to
revenge himself upon the Sioux for the death
of his son; but they knew that, whatever
his reason might be, it was not due to any
fear of the Sioux.   As time went on, they
thought that he would perhaps change his
mind, and again and again they came to him
begging for leave to take the war-path.   ' The
blood of your son,' they said, ' cries for revenge.   We have not ceased to weep for him
and for the other Frenchmen who were slain.
Give us permission and we will avenge their
death upon the Sioux.'

La Vérendrye, however, disregarding his
personal feelings, knew that it would be fatal
to all his plans to let the friendly Indians have

their way. An attack on the Sioux would be the signal for a general war among all the neighbouring tribes. In that case his forts would be destroyed and the fur trade would be broken up. In the end, he and his men would probably be driven out of the western country, and all his schemes for the discovery of the Western Sea would come to nothing. It was therefore of the utmost importance that he should remain where he was, in the country about the Lake of the Woods, until the excitement among the Indians had quieted down and there was no longer any immediate danger of war.

At length, in the summer of 1738, La Vérendrye felt that he could carry out his plan of visiting the Mandans. He left one of his sons, Pierre, in charge of Fort St Charles, and with the other two, François and Louis, set forth on his journey to the West. Travelling down the Winnipeg river in canoes, they stopped for a few hours at Fort Maurepas, then crossed Lake Winnipeg and paddled up the muddy waters of Red River to the mouth of the Assiniboine, the site of the present city of Winnipeg, then seen by white men for the first time. La Vérendrye found it occupied by a band of Crees under two war chiefs. He landed,

pitched his tent on the banks of the Assiniboine, and sent for the two chiefs and reproached them with what he had heard—that
they had abandoned the French posts and had
taken their furs to the English on Hudson Bay.
They replied that the accusation was false ;
that they had gone to the English during only
one season, the season in which the French had
abandoned Fort Maurepas after the death of
La Jemeraye, and had thus left the Crees with
no other means of getting the goods they required.   ' As long as the French remain on
our lands,' they said, ' we promise you not to
go elsewhere with our furs.'   One of the chiefs
then asked him where he was now going.
La Vérendrye replied that it was his purpose
to ascend the Assiniboine river in order to
see the country.   ' You will find yourself
among the Assiniboines,' said the chief ; ' and
they are a useless people, without intelligence,
who do not hunt the beaver, and clothe themselves only in the skins of buffalo.   They
are a good-for-nothing lot of rascals and
might do you harm.'   But La Vérendrye had
heard such tales before and was not to be
frightened from his purpose.   He took leave
of the Crees, turned his canoes up the shallow
waters of the Assiniboine river, and ascended

AN INDIAN ENCAMPMENT

From a painting by Paul Kane

it to where now stands the city of Portage
la Prairie. Here he built a fort, which he
named Fort La Reine, in honour of the queen
of France.

While this was being done, a party of
Assiniboines arrived. La Vérendrye soon
found, as he had expected, that the Crees
through jealousy had given the Assiniboines
a character which they did not deserve. With
all friendliness they welcomed the strangers
and were overjoyed at the presents which
the French gave them. The most valued
presents consisted of knives, chisels, awls, and
other small tools. Up to this time these people
had been dependent upon implements made
of stone and of bone roughly fashioned to serve
their purposes, and these implements were
very crude and inferior compared with the
sharp steel tools of the white men.

While La Vérendrye had been occupied in
building Fort La Reine, one of his men,
Louvière, had been sent to the mouth of the
Assiniboine to put up a small post for the
Crees. He found a suitable place on the south
bank of the Assiniboine, near the point where it
enters the Red, and here he built his trading
post and named it Fort Rouge. This fort
was abandoned in a year or two, as it was

soon found more convenient to trade with the Indians either at Fort Maurepas near the mouth of the Winnipeg, or at Fort La Reine on the Assiniboine. The memory of the fort is, however, preserved to this day. The quarter of Winnipeg in the vicinity of the old fort is still known as Fort Rouge. The memory of La Vérendrye is also preserved, for a large school built near the site of the old fort bears the name of the great explorer.

The completion of Fort La Reine freed La Vérendrye to make preparations for his journey to the Mandans. He left some of his men at the fort and selected twenty to accompany him on his expedition. To each of these followers he gave a supply of powder and bullets, an ax, a kettle, and other things needful by the way. In later years horses were abundant on the western prairie, but at that time neither the French nor the Indians had horses, and everything needed for the journey was carried on men's backs.

Three days after leaving Fort La Reine, La Vérendrye met a party of Assiniboines travelling over the prairie. He gave them some small presents, and told them that he had built in their country a fort where they could get all kinds of useful articles in ex-

change for their furs and provisions. They
seemed delighted at having white men so near,
and promised to keep the fort supplied with
everything that the traders required.

A day or two afterwards several other
Indians appeared, from an Assiniboine village.
They bore hospitable messages from the chiefs,
who begged the white travellers to come to
visit them. This it was difficult to do. The
village was some miles distant from the road
on which they were travelling, and already
they had lost much time because their guide
was either too lazy or too stupid to take
them by the most direct way to the Mandan villages on the banks of the Missouri.
Still, La Vérendrye did not think it wise to
disappoint the Assiniboines, or to offend them,
since he might have to depend upon their
support in making his plans for further discoveries. Accordingly, although it was now
nearly the middle of November, the very best
time of the year for travelling across the
plains, he made up his mind to go to the
Assiniboine village.

As the party drew near the village, a number
of young warriors came to meet them, and to
tell them that the Assiniboines were greatly
pleased to have them as guests. It is pos-

sible that the Assiniboines had heard of the
presents which the French had given to some
of their countrymen, and that they too hoped
to receive knives, powder and bullets, things
which they prized very highly.   At any rate,
the explorer and his men received vocifer-
ous welcome when they entered the village.
' Our arrival,' says La Vérendrye, ' was hailed
with great joy, and we were taken into the
dwelling of a young chief, where everything
had been made ready for our reception.   They
gave us and all our men very good cheer, and
none of us lacked appetite.'

The following day La Vérendrye sent for
the principal chiefs of the tribe, and gave to
each of them a present of powder and ball, or
knives and tobacco.   He told them that if the
Assiniboines would hunt beaver diligently and
would bring the skins to Fort La Reine, they
should receive in return everything that they
needed.   One of the chiefs made a speech in
reply.   ' We thank you,' he said, ' for the
trouble you have taken to come to visit us.
We are going to accompany you to the Mandans,
and then to see you safely back to your fort.
We have already sent word to the Mandans
that you are on your way to visit them, and
the Mandans are delighted.   We shall travel

AN ASSINIBOINE INDIAN

From a pastel by Edmund Morris

by easy marches, so that we may hunt by the way and have plenty of provisions.' The explorer was not wholly pleased to find that the entire village was to accompany him, for this involved still further delays on the journey. It was necessary, however, to give no cause of offence; so he thanked them for their good-will, and merely urged that they should be ready to leave as soon as possible and travel with all speed by the shortest road, as the season was growing late.

On the next morning they all set out to-gether, a motley company, the French with their Indian guides and hunters accompanied by the entire village of Assiniboines. La Vérendrye was astonished at the orderly way in which these savages, about six hundred in number, travelled across the prairies. Every-thing was done in perfect order, as if they were a regiment of trained soldiers. The warriors divided themselves into parties; they sent out scouts in advance to both the right and the left, in order to keep watch for enemies and also to look out for buffalo and other game; the old men marched in the centre with the women and the children; and in the rear was a strong guard of warriors. If the scouts saw buffalo ahead, they signalled to the rear-guard, who crept round the herd on both sides until it was surrounded. They killed as many buffaloes as were needed to provision the camp, and this completed the men's part of the work. It was the women who cut up the meat and carried it to the place where the company encamped for the night. The women, indeed, were the burden-bearers and had to carry most of the baggage. There were, of course, dogs in great numbers on such excursions, and these bore a part of the load. The men burdened themselves with nothing but their arms.

CHAPTER IV

THE MANDAN INDIANS

It was towards the end of November when La Vérendrye and his party reached the point where the Mandans had promised to meet them. When he arrived no one was on the spot; but presently, after he had encamped, a Mandan chief appeared with thirty followers. This chief advanced to La Vérendrye and presented him with Indian corn in the ear and with a roll of Indian tobacco. These were tokens of friendship. He told La Vérendrye how glad he and his countrymen were to welcome him to their villages, and begged him to consider the Mandans as his children.

La Vérendrye was surprised to find the appearance of the Mandans very much like that of the other tribes he had met. Stories told by the Crees and the Assiniboines had prepared him to find them of a different type, a type like that of the white men. In reality they looked like the Assiniboines and dressed in the same fashion. Their clothing was scanty enough, for it consisted of only a buffalo robe worn from the shoulders. It was clear now that the Indians had been telling him not what was true but what they thought he would like to hear. 'I knew then,' he says shrewdly, 'that a heavy discount must be taken off everything that an Indian tells you.'

The Mandan chief invited La Vérendrye to be his guest in the nearest village, and the whole party made ready to continue their journey to that point. Then the chief made a speech to the Assiniboines, very friendly in tone, but artfully intended to make them uneasy and send them back home. He was really anxious to have the white men as his guests, but he was not at all anxious to have as guests and to be obliged to feed an entire village of Assiniboines; and so, thinking to get rid of them, he played on their well-known fear of the fiery Sioux. 'We thank you,' he said to them, 'for having brought the French to see us. They could not have arrived at a better time. The Sioux are on the war-path, and may be here at any moment. We know the valour and courage of the French, and also of the Assiniboines, and we hope that you will both help us to defend ourselves from the Sioux.'

La Vérendrye was at first as much imposed upon by this story as were the Assiniboines, but with a very different effect. They were dismayed, while he rejoiced at the opportunity of having at last a fair chance to avenge the cruel death of his son. After the speech, the Mandan chief took him aside, and explained that the alarm was merely a trick to get rid of the Assiniboines. They had not food enough at the village, he said, to satisfy such a hungry horde. But, to the surprise and disgust of the chief, the Assiniboines swallowed their fears and decided to go forward. At first, in their terror, the majority of the tribe had thought it better to turn back; but one of their old chiefs shamed them into a different course. 'Do not think,' he said, in scornful accents, 'that our Father [La Vérendrye] is a coward,' and he looked about him at the young Assiniboine warriors until each felt that he himself was branded as a coward. 'I know him,' he continued, 'better than you do, and I tell you that the Sioux cannot frighten him or any of his men. What will he think of us? At our request, he went out of his way to visit our village. We promised to conduct him to the Mandans, and to bring him safely back to his fort. And now you talk of abandoning him, because you fear the Sioux. This must never be. Let those of you who are faint-hearted remain here in camp with the women; but let those who are without fear follow our father.' After this scornful eloquence there was no further talk of turning back.

Early on the following morning the camp broke up, and the whole party, French and Assiniboines and Mandans, marched across the plains towards the Mandan village. One can imagine the striking picture made up by the little party of white men in their picturesque costumes, surrounded by hundreds of half-naked savages. Had the Indians cared to exercise their power, they might have overwhelmed the French at any moment, but apparently they had no thought of doing so. Indeed it is quite true that the Indians of North America, when first they met white men, treated them in nearly every case with the utmost friendship. Only after the Indians had been deceived or betrayed by some rascals among the white men did they learn to look upon them as enemies and become cruel and treacherous in dealing with them.

When La Vérendrye had travelled some distance from the camp, he found that the bag containing his papers and many other things that would be required at the Mandan villages had been stolen by one of the Assiniboines. The thief, he also learned, had made off with his spoil.   Instantly he sent two young warriors to secure him.   The culprit was overtaken on the following day and the bag was recovered. The pursuers, however, instead of bringing it back to La Vérendrye, carried it on to their village to keep for him until his return.   This singular conduct was due to their fear of the Sioux.   The white man's bag would be safe at the Assiniboine village, but if they ventured to carry it back to La Vérendrye they were not so sure that either it or their own scalps would be safe at the Mandan village, with the ferocious Sioux hovering about.   They did not know, of course, that the story of the Sioux was nothing but a hoax.

When La Vérendrye arrived within a few miles of the Mandan village, he found awaiting him another party of Mandans under two of their chiefs.   They had lighted a camp-fire and had brought food for their guests.   The chiefs welcomed him, led him to the place of honour beside the fire, and presented him with some of their native dishes—corn pounded into a paste and baked in the coals and something

that looked like a pumpkin pie without the
pastry. The party smoked the pipe of peace
and carried on a rather clumsy conversation
by means of an interpreter. Then they resumed the journey and presently the Mandan
village appeared in sight. If the explorer had
been disappointed in finding the Mandans very
similar in appearance to other western tribes,
now at least he was gratified to find their
buildings more elaborate and interesting than
any he had before met with. The village was
in fact a fort, apparently strong enough to
protect the inhabitants from anything less
powerful than artillery, of which of course
they had no knowledge.

La Vérendrye, knowing that the Indians
were always impressed by an imposing ceremony, now drew up his men in military
order. He told his son François to march
in front, bearing the flag of France. The
Mandans, who looked upon the explorer as
a great white chief, would not permit him to
walk, but carried him upon their shoulders
to the gate of the fort. Naturally he did not
like this mode of travel, but he submitted to it
for fear of displeasing his hosts. As they drew
near the fort, he ordered his men to fire a
volley as a salute to the Mandans. The

principal chiefs and warriors flocked out to
meet him, and escorted him within their walls.
When he marched in with his force, he saw
the ramparts crowded with men, women, and
children, who looked with astonishment upon
the first white men they had ever seen. The
principal chief of the tribe led La Vérendrye
into his own lodge, and told him to consider
it his home so long as he cared to remain in
the village. When the two entered the lodge
a crowd of Mandans followed and the place
became suffocating. La Vérendrye told the
crowd that they should have many oppor-
tunities later to see him, and after some difficulty he managed to have the place cleared.

This, however, was not effected before the
unfortunate explorer had suffered another loss.
He found that, in the confusion, an enterprising Indian had snatched the bag of presents
from one of his men, and had made off with it.
This was serious. The bag contained nearly
all the gifts which he had brought for the
chiefs of the Mandans, and he feared that
these chiefs might now look coldly upon a
white man who was unable to offer the custom-
ary presents. He explained what had happened
to the principal chief. The chief seemed very
much put out and told La Vérendrye for his

consolation that there were a good many
rascals among the Mandans. Later, when
the Assiniboines told the chief that he was
himself the thief, he made the weak retort that
one of his accusers might be the culprit. He
promised to do his best to recover the bag, but
La Vérendrye never saw it again.

In a day or two the Assiniboines took
leave of La Vérendrye, and, much to the relief
of the Mandans, prepared to return to their
own village. Before their departure, the chief
of the Assiniboines made a speech to the
Mandans. 'We are leaving you our father,'
he said. 'Take great care of him, and of all
the French. Learn to know them, for they
are wise; they know how to do everything.
We love our father, and we also fear him. Do
as we do.' The Mandans promised to take
every care of the visitors. Everything the
village contained, they said, was at their
service for the asking. They begged that the
white chief would count them among the
members of his family. In compliance with
their wish, La Vérendrye went through the
usual ceremony of placing his hands on the
heads of each of the chiefs. By this ceremony
they became his 'children.' The Assiniboines,
though they had taken leave of La Vérendrye,

still delayed their departure. The Mandans, alarmed at the quantities of provisions their unwelcome guests required, again spread the report that the Sioux were approaching. Indeed, they said, several Mandan hunters had caught sight of them. This time the ruse succeeded. The Assiniboines, in a panic of alarm, marched off in great haste, lest the Sioux should intercept them before they could reach their own country.

Further troubles awaited La Vérendrye. The day following the departure of the Assiniboines he found that his Cree interpreter had gone off with them, although he had promised faithfully to remain. Even with this interpreter communications with the Mandans had been difficult. Before La Vérendrye's thoughts expressed in French could reach the Mandans, they had to pass through the medium of three other languages. One of La Vérendrye's sons, who understood Cree, was able to translate the explorer's questions into that language ; then the Cree interpreter put the questions into Assiniboine ; and several of the Mandans were sufficiently familiar with the language of the Assiniboines to complete the chain and express the ideas in their own tongue. With the Cree interpreter gone, the problem of communication became much more difficult. Indeed, the only method that remained of carrying on conversation with the Mandans was by means of signs and gestures.

One of La Vérendrye's principal reasons for visiting the Mandans had been to find out from them as much as possible of the country which lay westward. He had hoped that they would be able to tell him something definite about the Western Sea, something of the best way of reaching it, and of the tribes he should meet on the way. He had had very little time to put questions before his interpreter deserted, and now he feared that he should have to turn back, because he had no means of getting information from the Mandans. With a great deal of difficulty he managed to learn that there were six Mandan villages or forts, some on one side of the Missouri, some on the other, and that farther down this river lived two other tribes, the Panana and the Pananis, who were at war with the Mandans, although they had formerly been their fast friends. The Mandans told him by signs that as one went down the Missouri it became very wide, and that there a race dwelt who were white like himself. These people, they said, rode on horseback both when they hunted and when they went to war; they wore armour and fought with lances and sabres, which they handled with great skill. Their forts and houses were of stone and they cultivated their fields. A whole summer was necessary to reach their country from the Mandan villages.

La Vérendrye did not know how much of this to believe, and he was not even sure that he correctly understood what the Mandans tried to convey to him by signs. He was not at all certain that the quarter in which these people, so different from the Mandans, were said to live was the direction it was necessary to take in order to reach the Western Sea. He did not know the truth, that the river by which he stood, the Missouri, emptied into the Mississippi, and that the settlements spoken of by the Mandans were probably the Spanish settlements on the lower waters of the Mississippi. In order to extend his information, he used every agency to learn as much as possible about the Mandans themselves. He sent his son François to another village near by, to examine it and to make further inquiries.

La Vérendrye himself made close observations. He walked about the village in which he was quartered, and examined the fortifications with a great deal of interest. There were about one hundred and thirty cabins within the walls; the streets and squares were laid out regularly and were kept remarkably neat and clean. The smooth, wide ramparts were built of timber strengthened with cross-pieces. At each corner was a bastion, and the fort was surrounded by a ditch fifteen feet deep and from fifteen to eighteen feet wide. He was astonished to find such elaborate fortifications among a savage tribe. Nowhere else in the New World had he seen anything of the kind.

The dwellings of the Mandans were large and comfortable ; they were divided into several rooms and round the walls were beds in the form of bunks. They had earthen vessels in which they cooked their food. The women made very neat baskets of wicker-work. The most remarkable thing about these people was their prudence for the future. They had storerooms underground in which they stored the dressed skins which they preserved to trade with neighbouring tribes for guns and ammunition; they had products of Europe in use, though they had not yet come into direct contact with Europeans. In these storerooms they preserved also dried meat and grain for food in the winter. This foresight

impressed La Vérendrye. Most of the Indian
tribes lived only in the present ; when they had
food they feasted upon it from morning to
night, and when their provisions were gone
they starved. The Mandans, however, kept on
hand an ample supply of food, both for their
own use and for that of strangers who
might visit them. They amused themselves
with rude sports. Among these La Vérendrye
mentions a game of ball, but he does not
describe it. Probably it was the game of
lacrosse, which was played by many of the
Indian tribes long before white men came to
copy it from them.

After an absence of a few days, François
de La Vérendrye returned from the village
which he had visited. He had been warmly
welcomed. He reported that the village was
much larger than the one his father was living
in, and that it was fortified in the same way.
He had tried to question the Mandans of this
village, but could make nothing out of their
answers. They were so impatient to speak
that they would constantly interrupt one
another ; when asked about one thing they
would answer about another, because they did
not really understand the question. The
Mandans tried to make up in hospitality for

their inability to answer the Frenchman's
questions. ' As we found that it was a waste
of time to question them, we had to fall back
on feasting the whole time we were with them,
and even then we could not attend nearly
all the feasts to which we were invited.'

Early in December La Vérendrye decided
to leave the Mandans and to make the long
return journey to Fort La Reine. He now saw
that, even if he could gain useful information
from the Mandans about the nearest way to
the Western Sea, it would be impossible to
attempt the journey without a supply of
presents for the tribes he should meet. To
get these presents he must return to the
fort, but he would leave two of his men
with the Mandans for the winter, in order to
learn the language. Then, when he returned,
he would have interpreters upon whom he
could rely. When he told the Mandans by
signs that he must leave them, they seemed
sorry to lose him, and loaded him with provisions for his journey. They also promised
to take care of his two men during his absence.
He distributed among them all the small
articles which he had in his stores, particularly
the needles, which they highly prized. To the
principal chief he gave a flag, and a lead tablet

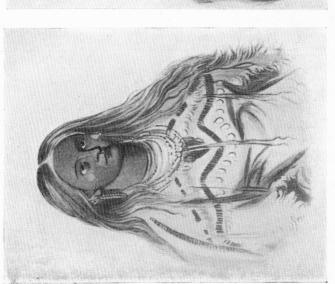

MANDAN GIRLS

From Prichard's *Natural History of Man*

bearing an inscription to the effect that he had taken possession of the Missouri country in the name of the king of France. This inscription the chief promised to preserve as his greatest treasure.

Misfortune, however, still dogged the path of La Vérendrye. The day before that on which he had arranged to leave for the north, he was taken violently ill and for three days could not move from his bed. As ill luck would have it, his stock of medicines was in the bag which the Assiniboines had carried off to their village, so that he could do nothing for himself until he reached that place. About the middle of December he was a little better, and made up his mind to attempt the journey. When he and his men set out on their long march across the plains, it was bitterly cold. They had no means of making a fire, and were compelled to sleep at night on the open prairie in a half-frozen condition. We can imagine what La Vérendrye must have suffered before at last he reached the Assiniboine village, more dead than alive. After a few days' rest, he managed to make his way slowly to Fort La Reine. ' Never in my life,' he says, ' did I endure so much misery, pain, and fatigue as on that journey.'

While at the Assiniboine village La Vérendrye reproached the Indians with having lied to him about the Mandans, so as to lead him to believe that they were white men. They replied that he had misunderstood them ; that they had not referred to the Mandans, but to another nation who lived farther down the river. One of the Assiniboines sprang up before him and exclaimed : ' I am the man best able to talk to you about this matter. Last summer I killed one of this nation of white men. He was covered with iron armour. If I had not killed his horse first, I should myself have been destroyed.' La Vérendrye asked him what he had brought back to prove his story. ' I had no chance to bring anything,' he said. ' When I was about to cut off his head, I saw some men on horseback, who were trying to prevent my retreat, and I had much difficulty in making my escape. I had to throw away everything I had, even to my blanket, and ran away naked.'

La Vérendrye thought that this man was probably telling the truth. What he said agreed fairly well with what he had himself heard from the Mandans, and was applicable probably to the Spaniards. But he was still as far away as ever from any direct information

about the road he should follow to reach the
Western Sea, and this was first and always
the thought that occupied his mind. He hoped
that the men whom he had left behind to
winter with the Mandans would be able to
obtain from them the facts for which he was
so anxiously waiting, and he looked forward
eagerly to the spring, when they were to return
to Fort La Reine with such news as they had
been able to gather.

CHAPTER V

THE DISCOVERY OF THE ROCKY MOUNTAINS

LA VÉRENDRYE had expected the return in the spring of 1739 of the two men whom he had left in the Mandan villages, but it was well into the autumn before they reached Fort La Reine. They brought good news, however. During the winter they had lost no opportunity of picking up Mandan words and phrases, until at last they were able to make themselves fairly well understood in that tongue. In the early summer a number of strange Indians had arrived from the West at the Mandan villages. They were on horseback, and brought with them many additional horses to carry their provisions and supplies. They came in order to trade embroidered buffalo hides and other skins with the Mandans for corn and beans, which they did not grow in their own country.

The young Frenchmen learned from the Mandans that a band of these Indians had their home in the extreme West, towards the setting sun. The Mandans also reported that in this country there were white men, who lived in brick and stone houses. In order to make further inquiries the two Frenchmen visited these Indians, and were fortunate enough to find among them a chief who spoke the language of the Mandans. He professed to speak also the language of the white men who dwelt in the West, but when the French heard this language they could make nothing of it. The chief declared that the strangers in his country wore beards and that in many other respects they resembled the white men. He declared that they prayed to the Master of Life in great buildings, where the Indians had seen them holding in their hands what, from their description, must have been books, the leaves like 'husks of Indian corn.' Their houses were described as standing near the shores of the great lake, whose waters rise and fall, and are unfit to drink. This would mean tides and salt water. If this Indian story was true, and there did not seem to be any reason for doubting it, La Vérendrye at last had something definite to guide him in his search for the Western Sea. He had but to find his way to the homes of these mysterious white strangers on its shores; and he hoped that the Indian band who had visited the Mandans, and from whom his men had obtained these particulars, would be able and willing to provide him with competent guides.

For some reason La Vérendrye was unable himself to return to the country of the Mandans or to go still farther west. But in the spring of 1740 he sent his eldest son Pierre into that country in order to make further inquiries, and to obtain guides if possible for the projected journey to the Western Sea. Pierre spent the following winter with the Mandans, but he could not find the men he needed as guides, and so he returned to Fort La Reine in the summer of 1741.

Not discouraged by this failure, François, who was known as the Chevalier, set out for the Mandans in the spring of 1742, accompanied by one of his brothers and by two men from the fort. The journey was to prove momentous, but at first difficulties beset the explorers. When they arrived in the Mandan country they could find no sign of the Horse Indians, as the mounted Indians from the West were called. François and his brother waited long at the Mandan village with what patience they could summon. The month of May went by, then June, then most of July, with still no sign of the missing band. Finally the brothers decided that, if they were to go farther west, they could wait no longer, for the season was advancing and it would soon be too late to do anything. At last they found among the Mandans two young men who agreed to lead them to the country of the Horse People. This would bring them to their hoped-for guides. Without a moment's delay they set out towards the south-west in search of the missing Indians.

They travelled for twenty days in a south-westerly direction, through what were afterwards known as the Bad Lands of the Little Missouri, a country unlike anything they had ever seen before. On every side they could see mounds and pillars of brilliantly-coloured earth, blue and crimson and green and yellow. So much were they struck with the singular spectacle that they would have liked to carry some of the coloured earth with them to show to their father on their return. But a long journey lay before them. They had to carry everything they needed on their backs, and it would have been folly to add to the load something that was useless for their immediate needs, something that they could neither eat nor wear.

About the beginning of August the party reached a mountain where the Mandans expected to find the Horse Indians so eagerly sought. But the Horse Indians had gone on a hunting expedition and had not yet returned; so François and his brother decided to wait for them. On the summit of the mountain they made a signal fire, and every day one of the explorers climbed up to the lookout to see if there were any signs of the Indians. At the foot of the mountain they built a small house in which they lived. Some of their time they spent in hunting to provision the camp, while waiting as patiently as they could for the Horse Indians to return from their hunting.

At last, on September 14, a smoke was seen rising in the south-western sky. One of the men was sent to investigate, and he found not the Horse Indians but a band known to the Mandans as the Good-looking Indians. Difficulties multiplied. One of the Mandan guides had already deserted them to go back to the Missouri, and the other now told the brothers that he must leave them. He was prompted by fear. The Good-looking Indians were not on friendly terms with the Mandans, and, although they had not offered to do him any harm, he was afraid to remain near these enemies.

After the Mandan had gone back, the brothers La Vérendrye managed to explain to the Good-looking Indians by signs that they were seeking the Horse Indians and asked for guides to one of the camps of these Indians. One of the Good-looking Indians said he knew the way, and they set out under his guidance; but they became anxious on finding that they were still travelling in the same direction as before, for this did not seem to be a very direct road to the Western Sea. Still, they had fixed their hopes on the Horse Indians as the people able to lead them there, and the most urgent thing to do was to find some members of that tribe, even though they had to go a long way out of their course to do so.

On the second day after they left the camp of the Good-looking Indians, they met a party of another tribe known as the Little Foxes, who were very friendly. The explorers gave them some small presents, and made them understand that they were seeking the Horse Indians, who had promised to show them the way to the sea. ‘ We will take you to the Horse Indians,’ they said, and their whole party turned about and joined the French. But these new guides also, to the disgust of François La Vérendrye,

still marched towards the south-west. ' I
felt sure,' he said, ' that in this direction we
should never find the Western Sea.' However,
there was nothing to do but to go forward, and
to trust to better luck after they reached the
Horse Indians.

After tramping on for many days they came
at last to an encampment of the Horse Indians.
These people, just then, were in great trouble.
They had been attacked not long before by a
war party of the Snake Indians ; many of their
bravest warriors had been killed, and many of
their women had been carried into captivity.
When asked the way to the sea these Indians
now declared that none of them had ever been
there, for the very good reason that the country
of the fierce Snake Indians must be crossed to
reach it. They said that a neighbouring tribe,
the Bow Indians, might be able to give some
information, as they either themselves traded
with the white men of the sea-coast, or were on
friendly terms with other tribes who had been
down to the sea. These Bow Indians, they
added, were the only tribe who dared to fight
against the Snake Indians, for they were under
the leadership of a wise and skilful chief, who
had more than once led his tribe to victory
against these dangerous enemies. A guide

was found to lead the explorers to the Bow Indians, and they went off once more, still travelling south - westerly, until at length, on November 21, they came in sight of the camp of the Bows. It was a huge camp, much larger than any the explorers had yet visited. Everywhere they could see numbers of horses, asses, and mules—animals unknown among the northern tribes.

When they reached the camp the chief of the Bows met them and at once took them to his own lodge. Nothing could be more friendly or polite than his treatment of the white travellers. In fact, as François said, he did not seem to have the manners of a savage. ' Up to that time we had always been very well received in the villages we had visited, but what we had before experienced in that way was nothing in comparison with the gracious manners of the head chief of the Bows. He took as much care of all our belongings as if they had been his own.' With him François and his brother remained for some time ; and, very soon, through the kindness of the chief, they learnt enough of the language to make themselves understood.

The explorers had many interesting talks with this friendly chief. They asked him if he

knew anything about the white people who
lived on the sea-coast. 'We know them,' he
replied, ' through what has been told us by
prisoners of the Snake tribe. We have never
been to the sea ourselves.' 'Do not be surprised,' he continued, ' to see so many Indians
camped round us. Word has been sent in all
directions to our people to join us here. In a
few days we shall march against the Snakes; and
if you will come with us, we will take you to the
high mountains that are near the sea. From
their summits you will be able to look upon
it.' The brothers La Vérendrye were overjoyed
to hear such encouraging news, and agreed that
one of them should accompany the Bow Indians
on their expedition against the Snakes. It
seemed almost too good to be true that they
might be actually within reach of the sea,
the goal towards which they and their father
had been struggling for so many years. In fact,
it proved too good to be true. Whether they
had misunderstood the chief, or whether he was
merely speaking from hearsay, certainly the
view was far from correct that the mountains
which they were approaching lay near the sea.
These mountains, not far off, were the Rocky
Mountains. Even if the explorers should
succeed in reaching and in crossing them at

this point, there would still be hundreds of miles of mountain forest and plain to traverse before their eyes could rest on the waters of the Pacific ocean. François and his brother never knew this, however, for they were not destined to see the western side of the mountains.

The great war party of the Bows, consisting of more than two thousand fighting men, with their families, started out towards the Snake country in December, the comparatively mild December of the south-western plains. The scene must have been singularly animated as this horde of Indians, with their wives and children, their horses and dogs, and the innumerable odds and ends that made up their camp equipage, moved slowly across the plains. François was too full of his own affairs to describe the odd appearance of this native army in the journal which he wrote of the expedition, but fortunately the historian Francis Parkman lived for some time among these tribes of the western plains, and he has given us a good idea of what such an Indian army must have looked like on the march. 'The spectacle,' he says, 'was such as men still young have seen in these western lands, but which no man will see again. The vast plain

swarmed with the moving multitude. The
tribes of the Missouri and the Yellowstone had
by this time abundance of horses, the best of
which were used for war and hunting, and the
others as beasts of burden. These last were
equipped in a peculiar manner. Several of the
long poles used to frame the teepees, or lodges,
were secured by one end to each side of a rude
saddle, while the other end trailed on the
ground. Crossbars lashed to the poles, just
behind the horse, kept them three or four feet
apart, and formed a firm support, on which was
laid, compactly folded, the buffalo-skin covering of the lodge. On this, again, sat a mother
with her young family, sometimes stowed for
safety in a large, open, willow basket, with the
occasional addition of some domestic pet—such
as a tame raven, a puppy, or even a small bear
cub. Other horses were laden in the same
manner with wooden bowls, stone hammers,
and other utensils, along with stores of dried
buffalo meat packed in cases of raw hide
whitened and painted. Many of the innumerable dogs—whose manners and appearance strongly suggested their relatives the
wolves, to whom, however, they bore a mortal
grudge—were equipped in a similar way, with
shorter poles and lighter loads. Bands of

naked boys, noisy and restless, roamed the
prairie, practising their bows and arrows on
any small animal they might find. Gay young
squaws—adorned on each cheek with a spot
of ochre or red clay and arrayed in tunics of
fringed buckskin embroidered with porcupine
quills—were mounted on ponies, astride like
men ; while lean and tattered hags—the
drudges of the tribe, unkempt and hideous—
scolded the lagging horses or screeched at
the disorderly dogs, with voices not unlike
the yell of the great horned owl. Most of
the warriors were on horseback, armed with
round white shields of bull hide, feathered
lances, war clubs, bows, and quivers filled
with stone-headed arrows ; while a few of
the elders, wrapped in robes of buffalo hide,
stalked along in groups with a stately air,
chatting, laughing, and exchanging unseemly
jokes.'

On the first day of January 1743, the
Indians, accompanied by the brothers La
Vérendrye and their Frenchmen, came within
sight of the mountains. Rising mysteriously
in the distance were those massive crags, those
silent, snow-capped peaks, upon which, as far
as we know, Europeans had never looked before.
The party of Frenchmen and Indians pressed

on, for eight days, towards the foot of the
mountains.   Then, when they had come within
a few days' journey of the place where they
expected to find the Snakes, they altered their
mode of advance.   It was now decided to leave
the women and children in camp under a small
guard, while the warriors pushed on in the hope
of surprising the Snakes in their winter camp
near the mountains.   While his brother remained in camp to look after the baggage of
the party, which the Indians would probably
pillage if left unguarded, François and his
two Frenchmen went forward with the war
party; and four days later they arrived at
the foot of the mountains, the first Europeans
who had ever put foot on those majestic
slopes.   François gazed with the keenest
interest at the lofty summits, and longed to
climb them to see what lay beyond.

Meanwhile he was obliged to share in a
vivid human drama.   The chief of the Bows
had sent scouts forward to search for the camp
of the Snakes, and these scouts now reappeared.
They had found the camp, but the enemy had
fled;   and had, indeed, gone off in such a
hurry that they had abandoned their lodges
and most of their belongings.   The effect pro-
duced by this news was singular.   Instead of

rejoicing because the dreaded Snakes had fled before them, which was evidently the case, the Bow warriors at once fell into a panic. The Snakes, they cried, had discovered the approach of their enemies, and must have gone back to attack the Bow camp and capture the women and children. The great chief tried to reason with his warriors; he pointed out that the Snakes could not know anything about the camp, that quite evidently they had been afraid to meet the Bows and had fled before them. But it was all to no purpose. The Bows would not listen to reason; they were sure that the Snakes had played them a cunning trick and that they should hasten back as speedily as possible to save their families. The result was characteristic of savage warfare. The Indian army that had marched a few days earlier in good order to attack the enemy now fled back along the trail in a panic, each man for himself.

It was in these ignominious circumstances that François La Vérendrye, having reached the foot of the Rocky Mountains, was obliged to turn back without going farther, leaving the mystery of the Great Sea still unsolved. François rode by the side of the disgusted chief and the two Frenchmen followed behind. Presently François noticed that his men had disappeared. He galloped back for some miles, and found them resting their horses on the banks of a river. While he talked with them, his quick eye detected the approach of a party of Snake Indians from a neighbouring wood. They were covering themselves with their shields, and were evidently bent on an attack. François and his men loaded their guns and waited until the Indians were well within range. Then they took aim and fired. The Snakes knew little or nothing about firearms, and when one or two of their number fell before this volley, they fled in disorder.

There was still danger of an attack by a larger band of the enemy, and the Frenchmen remained on guard where they were until nightfall. Then, under cover of darkness, they attempted to follow the trail of the Bows. But the ground was so dry and hard at that season of the year that they found it impossible to pick up the trail of their friends. For two days they wandered about. Skill or good fortune, however, aided them, and at last they arrived at the camp of the Bows, tired and half starved. The chief had been anxious at the disappearance of his white guests, and was overjoyed at their safe return. It is almost needless to say that the panic-stricken warriors

had found their camp just as they had left it;
no one had heard or seen anything of the
Snakes; and the warriors were forced to sub-
mit to the jeers of the squaws for their failure
to come even within sight of the enemy.

François, his brother, and their two men
accompanied the Bows for some days on their
homeward journey. They found, however,
that the Bows were travelling away from the
course which they wished to follow, and so
decided to leave them and to turn towards the
Missouri river. The chief of the Bows seemed
to feel genuine regret at bidding farewell to his
French guests, and he made them promise to
return and pay him another visit in the following spring, after they had seen their father at
Fort La Reine. On the long journey to this
point the three Frenchmen now set out across
the limitless frozen prairie.

About the middle of March they came upon
a party of strange Indians known as the People
of the Little Cherry. They were returning
from their winter's hunting, and were then
only two days' journey from their village on
the banks of the Missouri. Like all the other
tribes, the People of the Little Cherry received
the Frenchmen with perfect friendliness. The
party lingered with these Indians in their

village until the beginning of April, and
François spent most of his time learning their
language. This he found quite easy, perhaps
because he had already picked up a fair knowledge of the language of some of the neighbouring tribes, and it proved not unlike that of the
Little Cherry Indians. François found in the
village an Indian who had been brought up
among the Spaniards of the Pacific Coast, and
who still spoke their language as readily as
he spoke his mother tongue. He questioned
him eagerly about the distance to the Spanish
settlements and the difficulties of the way.
The man replied that the journey was long.
It was also, he said, very dangerous, because it
must be through the country of the Snake
Indians. This Indian assured François that
another Frenchman lived in the country where
they were, in a village distant about three
days' journey. Naturally this surprised
François and his brother. They thought of
going to visit him; but their horses were
badly in need of a rest after the long trip
from the mountains, and must be kept fresh
for the journey to the Mandan villages. They
therefore sent instead a letter to the Frenchman, asking him to visit them at the village of
the Little Cherries, or, if that was not possible,

at least to send them an answer. No answer came, and we may well doubt whether such a Frenchman existed. Before leaving the country, La Vérendrye buried on the summit of a hill a tablet of lead, with the arms and inscription of the French king. This was to take possession of the country for France. He also built a pyramid of stones in honour of the governor of Canada.[1]

About the beginning of April, when the horses were in good condition and all preparations had been made for the journey, the explorers said good-bye to the People of the Little Cherry and set out for the Mandan villages. Like the Bow Indians, the Little Cherries seemed sorry to lose them and begged them to come back. In return for the kindness and hospitality he had received, La Vérendrye distributed some presents and promised to visit them again when he could.

On May 18 the travellers reached the

[1] This tablet remained buried where it was deposited for 170 years. In March 1913 it was found by a young girl on the west bank of the Missouri river opposite the city of Pierre, S. Dakota, thus bearing testimony to the trustworthiness of François La Vérendrye's journal, from which this chapter was written before the tablet was discovered. Photographs of the tablet were made by W. O'Reilly of Pierre and published in the *Manitoba Free Press* and are reproduced in this book by courtesy of Charles N. Bell, F.R.G.S., of Winnipeg.

Mandan villages and were welcomed as if they had returned from the dead. Their long absence had led the Mandans to conclude that they had been killed by some unfriendly Indians, or that some fatal accident had happened on the way. They had intended to rest for some time at the Mandan villages, but they found that a party of Assiniboines was going to Fort La Reine, and they determined to travel with them. The Assiniboines had in fact already left on their journey, but the Frenchmen overtook them at their first camp.

This latter part of the journey had its own excitements and perils. On the last day of May, as they were travelling over the prairie, they discovered a party of Sioux waiting in ambush. The Sioux had expected to meet a smaller party, and now decided not to fight. At the same time, they were too proud to run away before the despised Assiniboines, even though they numbered only thirty and the Assiniboines numbered more than a hundred. They retreated with dignified slowness, facing around on the Assiniboines from time to time, and driving them back when they ventured too near. But when they recognized the French-men, mounted on horses and armed with their deadly muskets, their attitude changed; they

TABLET DEPOSITED BY LA VÉRENDRYE, 1743
Obverse and reverse sides

From photographs lent by Charles N. Bell, F.R.G.S., President
of the Manitoba Historical and Scientific Society

forgot their dignity and made off as fast as they could go. Even with heavy odds against them these virile savages managed to wound several of the Assiniboines, while they lost only one man, who mistook the enemy for his friends and was captured. The brothers La Vérendrye finally reached Fort La Reine on July 2, to the great delight of their father, who had grown anxious on account of their long absence. They had been away from the fort for one year and eighty-four days.

CHAPTER VI

LA VÉRENDRYES' LATTER DAYS

DURING all this time the elder La Vérendrye had been working at other plans for discovery and for trade in the Far West. In the year 1739, on his return from the first visit to the Mandans, he had sent his son François to build a fort on the Lake of the Prairies, now known as Lake Manitoba. When young La Vérendrye had built this fort, he went farther north to Cedar Lake, near the mouth of the Saskatchewan river, and there built another fort. The purpose was to intercept the trade of the Indians with the English on Hudson Bay. For over half a century the Indians of this region had taken their furs down the rivers leading from Lake Winnipeg to the trading-posts of the Hudson's Bay Company on the shores of the Bay, but now the French intended to offer them a market nearer home and divert to themselves this profitable trade. The first of their new forts was named Fort Dauphin, and the one on Cedar Lake was called Fort Bourbon.

Having built Fort Bourbon, François La Vérendrye had ascended the Saskatchewan river as far as the Forks, where the north and south branches of that great river join. Here he met a number of Crees, whom he questioned as to the source of the Saskatchewan. They told him that it came from a great distance, rising among lofty mountains far to the west, and that beyond those mountains they knew of a great lake, as they called it, the water of which was not good to drink. The mountains were of course the Rocky Mountains, and the waters of the great lake which the Crees spoke of were the salt waters of the Pacific ocean. François La Vérendrye had continued his work of building forts. Shortly after building Fort Bourbon, he built Fort Paskoyac, on the Saskatchewan, at a place now known as the Pas, between Cedar Lake and the Forks. It is interesting to know that a railway has just been completed to this place, and that it is to be continued from there to the shores of Hudson Bay. How this modern change would have startled the old fur-traders! Even if they could have dreamed of anything so wonderful as a railway, we can imagine their ridicule of the idea that some day men should travel from the East to the far-off shores of the Saskatchewan in two or three days, a trip which cost them months of wearisome paddling.

In carrying on his work in the West, La Vérendrye had to face difficulties even greater than those caused by the hard life in the wilderness. His base of supplies was in danger. He had many enemies in Canada, who took advantage of his absence in the West to prejudice the governor against him. They even sent false reports to the king of France, saying that he was spending his time, not in searching for a way to the Western Sea, but in making money out of the fur trade. This was not true. Not only was he making no money out of the fur trade, but, as we have seen, he was heavily in debt because of the enormous cost of carrying on his explorations. For a time, however, the truth did not help him. The tales told by his enemies were believed, and he was ordered to return to Montreal with his sons. He and they withdrew from their work in the West, left behind their promising beginnings, and returned to the East. Never again, as it happened, was the father to resume his work. Another officer, M. de Noyelle, was sent to the West to continue the work of exploration. Noyelle spent two years in the West without

adding anything to the information La Vérendrye had gained. By that time a natural re-
action had come in favour of La Vérendrye, and
the acting governor of Canada, the Marquis de
La Galissonière, decided to put the work of
exploration again in charge of La Vérendrye
and his sons. In recognition of his services
he was given the rank of captain and was
decorated with the Cross of St Louis.

While these events were ripening, the years
passed, and not until 1749 was La Vérendrye
restored to his leadership in the West. Though
now sixty-four years old, he was overjoyed at
the prospect. Not only was he permitted to
continue his search for the Western Sea ;
the quality of his work was recognized, for the
governor and the king had at last understood
that, instead of seeking his own profit in his
explorations, as his enemies had said, he had
the one object of adding to the honour and
glory of his country. He made preparations
to start from Montreal in the spring of 1750,
and intended to push forward as rapidly as
possible to Fort Bourbon, or Fort Paskoyac,
where he would spend the winter. In the
spring of the following year he would ascend
the Saskatchewan river and make his way
over the mountains to the shores of the Western

Sea, the Pacific ocean as we know it to-day.
But the greatest of all enemies now blocked
his way. La Vérendrye was taken ill while
making his preparations for the expedition,
and before the close of the year 1749 he had
set out on the journey from which no man
returns.

After the death of La Vérendrye, his sons
made preparations to carry out his plan for
reaching the Western Sea by way of the Saskatchewan river. They had the same un-
selfish desire to bring honour to their king and
to add new territories to their native land.
Moreover, this project, which their father had
had so much at heart, had become now for
them a sacred duty. To their dismay, however, they soon found that the promise made
to their father did not extend to themselves.
Another officer, Legardeur de Saint-Pierre, was
appointed by the governor of Canada to carry on
the search for the Western Sea. They had spent
years of toil and discomfort in the wilderness
and endured countless hardships and dangers.
They had carefully studied the languages,
manners, and customs of the Indian tribes,
and they had found out by hard experience what
would be the best means of completing their
discovery. Yet now they were thrown aside in

THE MARQUIS DE LA GALISSONIÈRE
From an engraving in the Château de Ramezay

favour of an officer who had never been in the
Far West and who knew nothing of the conditions he would there be compelled to meet.

They could at least appeal for justice. In
a last attempt to obtain this for himself and
his brothers, François de La Vérendrye wrote
this letter to the king's minister :

The only resource left to me is to throw
myself at the feet of your Lordship and to
trouble you with the story of my misfortunes. My name is La Vérendrye ; my
late father is known here [in Canada] and in
France by the exploration for the discovery
of the Western Sea to which he devoted
the last fifteen years of his life. He
travelled and made myself and my brothers
travel with such vigour that we should
have reached our goal, if he had had only
a little more help, and if he had not been
so much thwarted, especially by envy.
Envy is still here, more than elsewhere, a
prevailing passion against which one has
no protection. While my father, my
brothers, and myself were exhausting ourselves with toil, and while we were incurring
a crushing burden of expense, his steps and
ours were represented as directed only
towards [our own gain by] the finding of

beaver ; the outlay he was forced to incur was described as dissipation ; and his narratives were spoken of as a pack of lies. Envy as it exists in this country is no half envy ; its principle is to calumniate furiously in the hope that if even half of what is said finds favour, it will be enough to injure. In point of fact, my father, thus opposed, had to his sorrow been obliged more than once to return and to make us return because of the lack of help and protection. He has even been reproached by the court [for not giving adequate reports upon his work] ; he was, indeed, more intent on making progress than on telling what he was doing until he could give definite statements. He was running into debt, he failed to receive promotions. Yet his zeal for his project never slackened, persuaded as he was that sooner or later his labours would be crowned with success and recompense.

At the time when he was most eager in the good work, envy won the day, and he saw the posts he had established and his own work pass into other hands. While he was thus checked in his operations, the reward of a plentiful harvest of beaver skins [which he had made possible] went

to another rather than himself. Yet [in
spite of this profitable trade the good work
slackened] ; the posts, instead of multi-
plying, fell into decay, and no progress was
made in exploration ; it was this, indeed,
which grieved him the most.

Meanwhile the Marquis de la Galissonière
arrived in the country [to act as governor].
In the hubbub of contradictory opinions
that prevailed, he came to the conclusion
that the man who had pursued such discoveries at his own charge and expense,
without any cost to the king, and who had
gone into debt to establish useful posts,
merited better fortune. Apart from advancing the project of discovery, practical
services had been rendered. There was
[the marquis reported] a large increase
of beaver in the colony, and four or five
posts had been well-established, and defended by forts as good as could be made
in countries so distant ; a multitude of
savages had been turned into subjects of
the king; some of them, in a party which
I commanded, showed an example to our
own domiciled savages by striking at the
Anniers Indians, who are devoted to
England. Progress [the marquis con-
cluded] could be hastened and rendered

more efficacious only by allowing the work to remain in the same hands.

Thus it was that the Marquis de la Galissonière was good enough to explain his position. No doubt he expressed himself to the court to a similar effect, for in the following year, that is to say last year, my father was honoured with the Cross of St Louis, and was invited to continue with his sons the work which he had begun. He made arrangements with great earnestness for starting on his expedition; he spared nothing that might make for success; he had already bought and prepared all the goods to be used in trade; he inspired me and my brothers with his own ardour. Then in the month of December last death carried him off.

Great as was my grief at the time, I could never have imagined or foreseen all that I lost in losing him. When I succeeded to his engagements and his responsibilities, I ventured to hope that I should succeed to the same advantages. I had the honour to write on the subject to the Marquis de la Jonquière [then governor], informing him that I had recovered from an indisposition from which I had been suffering, and which might serve as a pretext to some one seeking to supplant me. His reply was that he had chosen Monsieur de Saint-Pierre to go to the Western Sea.

I started at once for Quebec from Montreal, where I then was ; I represented the situation in which I was left by my father ; I declared that there was more than one post in the direction of the Western Sea and that I and my brothers would be delighted to be under the orders of Monsieur de Saint-Pierre, and that we could content ourselves, if necessary, with a single post, and that the most distant one; I stated that we even asked no more than leave to go on in advance [of the new leader], so that while we were pushing the work of exploration, we might be able to help ourselves by disposing of my father's latest purchases and of what remained to us in the posts. We should in this have the consolation of making our utmost efforts to meet the wishes of the court.

The Marquis de la Jonquière, though he felt the force of my representations, and, as it seemed to me, was touched by them, told me at last that Monsieur de Saint-Pierre did not wish for either me or my brothers. I asked what would become of the debts we had incurred. Monsieur de Saint-Pierre, however, had spoken, and I could not obtain anything. I returned to Montreal with this not too consoling information. There I offered for sale a small piece of property, all that I had inherited from my father. The proceeds of this sale served to satisfy my most urgent creditors.

Meanwhile the season was advancing. There was now the question of my going as usual to the rendezvous arranged with my hired men, so as to save their lives [by bringing provisions], and to secure the stores which, without this precaution, would probably be pillaged and abandoned. In spite of Monsieur de Saint-Pierre, I obtained permission to make this trip, and I was subject to conditions and restrictions such as might be imposed on the commonest voyageur. Nevertheless, scarcely had I left when Monsieur de Saint-Pierre complained of my action and alleged that this start of mine before him injured him to the amount of more than ten thousand francs. He also accused me, without the slightest reserve, of having loaded my canoe beyond the permission accorded me.

The accusation was considered and my canoe was pursued ; had I been overtaken at once, Monsieur de Saint-Pierre would have been promptly reassured. He overtook me at Michilimackinac, and if I can believe what he said, he now saw that he had been in the wrong in acting as he did, and was vexed with himself for not having taken me and my brothers with him. He expressed much regret to me and paid me many compliments. It may be that this is his usual mode of acting; but it is difficult for me to recognize in it either good faith or humanity.

Monsieur de Saint-Pierre might have obtained all that he has obtained; he might have made sure of his interests and have gained surprising advantages; and have taken [as he desired] some relative with him while not shutting us out entirely. Monsieur de Saint-Pierre is an officer of merit, and I am only the more to be pitied to find him thus turned against me. Yet in spite of the favourable impressions he has created on different occasions, he will find it difficult to show that in this matter he kept the main interest [that of discovery] in view, and that he conformed to the intentions of the court and respected the kindly disposition with which the Marquis de la Galissonière honours us. Before

such a wrong could be done to us, he must
have injured us seriously in the opinion
of Monsieur de la Jonquière, who himself is
always disposed to be kind.

None the less am I ruined. My returns
for this year were only half collected, and
a thousand subsequent difficulties make the
disaster complete ; with credit gone in re-
lation both to my father and to myself, I
am in debt for over twenty thousand francs ;
I remain without funds and without patri-
mony. Moreover, I am a simple ensign of
the second grade ; my elder brother has
only the same rank as myself, while my
younger brother is only a junior cadet.

Such is the net result of all that my
father, my brothers, and I have done. The
one who was murdered some years ago was
not the most unfortunate of us. His blood
does not count in our behalf. Unless Monsieur de Saint-Pierre becomes imbued with
better sentiments and communicates them
to the Marquis de la Jonquière, all my
father's toils and ours fail to serve us, and
we must abandon what has cost us so much.
We certainly should not have been and
should not be useless to Monsieur de Saint-
Pierre. I explained to him fully how I
believed I could serve him ; clever as he

may be, and inspired with the best intentions, I venture to say that by keeping us away he is in danger of making many mistakes and of getting often on the wrong track. It is something gained to have gone astray, but to have found out your error ; we think that now we should be sure of the right road to reach the goal, whatever it may be. It is our greatest cause of distress to find ourselves thus snatched away from a sphere of action in which we were proposing to use every effort to reach a definite result.

Deign therefore, Monseigneur, to judge the cause of three orphans. Our misfortune is great, but is it without remedy ? There are in the hands of your Lordship resources of compensation and of consolation, and I venture to hope for some benefit from them. To find ourselves thus excluded from the West would be to find ourselves robbed in the most cruel manner of our heritage. We should have had all that was bitter and others all that was sweet.

This eloquent appeal of François fell upon unheeding ears ; the appointment of his rival was confirmed. The only grace he could obtain was leave to take to the West a small portion of the supplies for which he and his brothers had already paid, and to return with the furs his men had collected and brought down to Michilimackinac. Thus ended, sadly enough, the devoted efforts of this remarkable family of explorers to complete the long search for a route overland to the Pacific ocean. The brothers La Vérendrye, ruined in purse and denied opportunity, fell into obscurity and were forgotten.

It remains only to tell briefly of the attempts of Saint-Pierre and his men to carry out the same great project. In obedience to the governor's instructions, Saint-Pierre left Montreal in the spring of 1750. He paddled up the Ottawa, and then through Lake Nipissing, and down the French river to Georgian Bay. He crossed Lake Huron to Michilimackinac, where he remained for a short time to give his men a rest. Then he pushed on to Grand Portage, where he spent some time in talking to the Indians. In spite of his ungenerous treatment of the sons of La Vérendrye, Saint-Pierre was a brave and capable soldier ; but he knew very little of the hardships of western exploration, or of the patience needed in dealing with Indians. He grumbled bitterly about the difficulties and hardships of the portages, which La Vérendrye had taken as a matter of course; and, instead of treating the Indians with patience and forbearance, he lost no opportunity to harangue and scold them. We need not wonder, therefore, that the natives, who had looked up to La Vérendrye as a superior being, soon learned to dislike the overbearing Saint-Pierre, and would do nothing to help him in his attempts at exploration.

Saint-Pierre visited Fort St Charles; he spent the winter at Fort Maurepas; in the spring of 1751 he went on to Fort La Reine. Meanwhile he had sent Niverville, a young officer of his party, to the Saskatchewan river, with instructions to push his discoveries westward beyond the farthest point reached by La Vérendrye. Winter had set in before Niverville set out on his long journey, and he travelled over the snow and ice with snow-shoes, dragging his provisions on toboggans. He knew nothing of the Indian method of harnessing dogs to their toboggans, and he and his men dragged the toboggans themselves. He travelled slowly across Lake Winnipeg, over rough ice and through deep snowdrifts, with no protection from the bitter winds. So great were the hardships that, in the end, he was compelled to abandon some of the heavier supplies and provisions. Before he and his men reached Fort Paskoyac they were at the point of starvation. During the last few days they had nothing to eat but a few small fish caught through holes in the ice.

Niverville was taken seriously ill, and had to remain at Fort Paskoyac, while some of his men in the spring of 1751 ascended the Saskatchewan in canoes. These men, we are told, paddled up the river to the foot of the Rocky Mountains, where they built a fort, named Fort La Jonquière, in honour of the governor. Later in the year Niverville followed his men up the river. At Fort La Jonquière he met a party of Western Indians, who told him that in the course of a war expedition they had encountered a number of Indians of a strange tribe carrying loads of beaver skins. These strange Indians told the Frenchmen that they were on their way over the Rocky Mountains to trade their furs with white men on the sea-coast. For some reason, either through lack of supplies or because he did not possess the courage and enthusiasm which had carried the La Vérendryes through so many difficulties, Niverville made no effort to cross the mountains. This attempt to reach the Western Sea ended, so far as French explorers were concerned, at Fort La Jonquière. All the toils and hardships of the French explorers ended in failure to achieve the great end at which they aimed. Members of another race reaped the coveted reward. Many years later a Scottish-Canadian explorer, Alexander Mackenzie, realized La Vérendrye's dream by successfully crossing the Rocky Mountains and forcing his way through the difficult country that lay beyond, until at last he stood upon the shores of the Pacific ocean.

Meanwhile Saint-Pierre had remained at Fort La Reine, leaving the work of exploration to his young lieutenant, Niverville. One incident of his life there remains to be described before we close this story of the search for the Western Sea. It cannot be better told than in Saint-Pierre's own narrative :

On February 22, 1752 [he says], about nine o'clock in the morning, I was at this post with five Frenchmen. I had sent the rest of my people, consisting of fourteen persons, to look for provisions, of which I had been in need for several days. I was sitting quietly in my room, when two hundred Assiniboines entered the fort, all of them armed. These Indians scattered immediately all through the place ; several of them even entered my room, but unarmed; others remained in adjacent parts of the fort. My people came to warn me of the behaviour of these Indians. I ran to them and told them sharply that they were very impudent to come in a crowd to my house, and armed. One of them answered in the Cree language that they came to smoke. I told them that they were not behaving properly, and that they must leave the fort at once. I believe that the firmness with which I spoke somewhat frightened them, especially as I put four of the most resolute out of the door, without their saying a word.

I went at once to my room. At that very moment, however, a soldier came to tell me that the guard-house was full of Indians, who had taken possession of the arms. I ran to the guard-house and demanded, through a Cree interpreter, what they meant by such behaviour. During all this time I was preparing to fight them with my weak force. My interpreter, who proved a traitor, said that these Indians had no bad intentions. Yet, a moment before, an Assiniboine orator, who had been constantly making fine speeches to me, had told the interpreter that, in spite of him, the Indians would kill and rob me.

When I had barely made out their intentions I failed to realize that I ought to have taken their arms from them. [To frighten them] I seized hold of a blazing brand, broke in the door of the powder magazine, and knocked down a barrel of gunpowder. Over this I held the brand, and I told the Indians in an assured tone [through the interpreter] that I expected nothing at their hands, and that even if I was killed I should have the glory of subjecting them to the same fate. No sooner had the Indians seen the lighted brand, and the barrel of gunpowder with its head staved in, and heard my interpreter, than they all fled out of the gate of the fort. They damaged the gate considerably in their hurried flight. I soon laid down my brand, and then I had nothing more exciting to do than to close the gate of the fort.

Soon after this incident with the Assiniboines, Saint-Pierre gave up his half-hearted attempt to find a route to the Western Sea, and returned to Montreal. He had proved himself a brave man enough. He did not, however, understand, and made no attempt to understand, the character of the Indians, and, as an explorer, he was a complete failure. In a couple of years he managed to undo all the work which La Vérendrye had accomplished. After he abandoned the West, the forts which had been built there with such difficulty and at such great expense soon fell into decay. The only men who had the knowledge and the enthusiasm to make real La Vérendrye's dream of exploration, his own sons, were denied the privilege of doing so; and no one else seemed anxious even to attempt such a difficult task.

The period of French rule in Canada was now rapidly drawing to a close. Instead of adding to the territories of France in North America, her sons were preparing to make their last stand in defence of what they already possessed. Half a dozen years later their dream of western exploration, and of a great North American empire reaching from the Atlantic to the Pacific, came to an end on the Plains of Abraham. It was left for those of another race who came after them to turn the dream of their rivals into tangible achievements. It must never be forgotten, however, that, although Pierre de La Vérendrye failed to complete the great object of his ambition, we owe to him and his gallant sons the discovery of a large part of what is to-day Western Canada.

BIBLIOGRAPHICAL NOTE

AN English translation of *The Journals of La
Vérendrye* edited by Lawrence J. Burpee, with
the French text, will be found among the pub-
lications of the Champlain Society. The
reader should consult also Parkman, *A Half
Century of Conflict*, chapter xvi.; Burpee,
The Search for the Western Sea; Shortt and
Doughty (editors), *Canada and its Provinces*,
vol. i., 'The Pathfinders of the Great West.'

INDEX

Printed by T. and A. Constable, Printers to His Majesty
at the Edinburgh University Press

CHRONICLES OF CANADA

Edited by George M. Wrong and H. H. Langton
of the University of Toronto

A series of thirty-two tersely-written narratives for popular reading, designed to set forth, in historic continuity, the principal events and movements in Canada, from the Earliest Explorers to the Railway Builders.

Chronicles of Canada

* NOTE.—The eight volumes marked with an asterisk are still in preparation and subject to changes in authorship should unforeseen circumstances prevent any author from completing his manuscript.

Published by
Glasgow, Brook & Company
at 15 Wilton Avenue
TORONTO, CANADA